Human Rights

Also by Peter R. Baehr

DE RECHTEN VAN DE MENS: Universaliteit in de Praktijk

DE VERENIGDE NATIES: Ideaal en Werkelijkheid

MENSENRECHTEN: Bestanddeel van het Buitenlands Beleid

POLICY ANALYSIS AND POLICY INNOVATION (*with Björn Wittrock*)

*THE ROLE OF HUMAN RIGHTS IN FOREIGN POLICY

THE NETHERLANDS AND THE UNITED NATIONS: Selected Issues (*editor with Monique Castermans-Holleman*)

THE UNITED NATIONS: Reality and Ideal (*with Leon Gordenker*)

*THE UNITED NATIONS AT THE END OF THE 1990s (*with Leon Gordenker*)

from the same publishers

Human Rights

Universality in Practice

Peter R. Baehr
Emeritus Professor of Human Rights
Utrecht University and Leiden University
The Netherlands

First published in hardcover 1999

First published in paperback 2001 by PALGRAVE
Houndmills, Basingstoke, Hampshire RG21 6XS and
175 Fifth Avenue, New York, N. Y. 10010
Companies and representatives throughout the world

PALGRAVE is the new global academic imprint of
St. Martin's Press LLC Scholarly and Reference Division and
Palgrave Publishers Ltd (formerly Macmillan Press Ltd).

ISBN 0–333–76314–9 hardback (*outside North America*)
ISBN 0–312–22180–0 hardback (*in North America*)
ISBN 0–333–96856–5 paperback (*worldwide*)

This book is printed on paper suitable for recycling and
made from fully managed and sustained forest sources.

A catalogue record for this book is available
from the British Library.

The Library of Congress has cataloged the hardcover edition as follows:
Baehr, P. R. (Peter R.)
   [Rechten van de mens. English]
   Human rights: universality in practice / Peter R. Baehr
      p. cm.
   Translation of: De rechten van de mens.
   Includes bibliographical references (p.) and index.
   ISBN 0–312–22180–0 (cloth)
    1. Human rights. I. Title.
   JC571.B3213 1999
   341.4'81—dc21   98–55203
                                             CIP

10 9 8 7 6 5 4 3 2 1
10 09 08 07 06 05 04 03 02 01

Printed and bound in Great Britain by
Antony Rowe Ltd, Chippenham, Wiltshire

For Malie

Contents

Preface to the Paperback Edition

What was said in the first, hardcover edition of this book remains substantially unchanged. Yet, a number of developments have occurred in the meantime which tend to emphasize some of the points then made. The fiftieth anniversary of the Universal Declaration of Human Rights (1998) served to underline its continuing importance as a 'common standard of achievement for all peoples and all nations', as worded in its preamble. These standards of human rights are as important as when they were first proclaimed, but their practical implementation worldwide remains a matter of continuing concern. Both at the regional and at the international levels, far too little personnel and finances are made available for the international supervision of these norms. This was one of the very reasons given by the widely respected UN High Commissioner for Human Rights, Mary Robinson, in the spring of 2001 for not seeking a second term of office. At the regional level, the European and American systems of supervision are still more effective than the African one, while Asia continues to lack any system of regional supervision.

The issue of collective rights is still on the international political agenda. Such questions as the rights of peoples – whether indigenous or not – are hotly debated. These are closely related to questions involving the right of peoples, as well as individuals, to a clean and healthy environment, both for themselves and for their offspring. The states of the world, sometimes erroneously referred to as the 'international community', find it hard to opt for long-term interests such as a sustained development, when there are seemingly attractive short-term options available. The human rights of collectivities do often not coincide with the national interests of states and tend to be on the losing side, at least for the time being.

Much lip service is being paid, both by western as well as non-western governments to the importance of implementing not only civil and political rights but economic, social and cultural rights as well. It seems almost in vain that in 1993 the World Conference on Human Rights in Vienna proclaimed that equal attention should be given to 'all' human rights. It is to be greatly regretted that no government – not even the ones that claim to be genuinely committed to human rights – has so far taken the initiative to recommend the adoption of an individual complaints procedure in this field. The United States of America may be the least hypocritical in that it has openly rejected recognition of economic, social and cultural rights as human rights. However, that is probably the most positive thing that can be said about the US position. How can one reject such notions as the rights to food, shelter, clothing, and health, yet continue to accept the right to life as a human right?

The United States further distinguishes itself in the sense that the majority of its states continue to accept and practice the death penalty as a valid punishment, in spite of its basic incompatibility with the right to life as well as its incorrigibility in the face of often made mistakes. Even worse: when becoming a party to the International Covenant on Civil and Political Rights, it rejected the prohibition on imposing the death penalty on minors. China and many other countries join the United States in this mistaken view of what the right to life should mean.

All human rights are still being violated all over the world. Countries such as Afghanistan, China, Burma, Iran, Iraq, Burundi, Congo, Sierra Leone, and the Russian Federation are among the worst, but certainly not the only offenders. Non-governmental organizations continue their uphill struggle to call attention to these abuses. They sometimes have some measure of success in their 'mobilization of shame'. Although the results achieved by their efforts may often be less than desirable, one should remember that in the absence of these efforts, the situation would certainly not be better.

'Humanitarian intervention' is a term that received notoriety when the NATO air strikes were carried out on Kosovo. The air strikes were a response to the gross violations of the human rights of ethnic Albanians by Yugoslav military and police forces, causing many of them to flee to the neighbouring countries of Albania and Macedonia. The question was and still is hotly debated whether the Security Council should have been involved and whether in the absence of Security Council authorization such military intervention should be allowed. It would seem fair to argue that, while dubious from a legal point of view, such actions may be politically acceptable, if they are the only remaining mechanisms to prevent or put an end to gross human rights violations. However, it goes without saying that common criteria must be developed so as to prevent states from resorting to 'humanitarian intervention' whenever it happens to suit their foreign policy purposes.

The issue of how to deal with past abuses of human rights and international humanitarian law is receiving a great deal of public as well as scholarly attention. In more than 20 countries so-called truth and reconciliation commissions have dealt with this issue, the one in South

Africa being the largest and most successful as well as most controversial operation of them all. The request by a Spanish judge to the United Kingdom to extradite the former Chilean dictator Augusto Pinochet – though unsuccessful in the end – has provided a clear and unmistakable message to other political leaders of his kind. It also served to revive the debate in his home country about the possibility of having him tried by a Chilean court. The tribunals on Yugoslavia and Rwanda continue to make a contribution to combating impunity at a slow, but irrepressible pace. The fact that persons from the former Yugoslavia who have been indicted, surrender themselves voluntarily to the Tribunal, is a welcome development, reflecting its growing authority. Yet, at the time of writing, some major culprits still have refrained from following this example. Finally, the Statute of the International Criminal Court has now been adhered to by some 30 states. When another 30 states have done so too, the Court will come into being which should serve as another powerful message to those responsible for gross human rights violations, while hopefully deterring others from doing the same.

The role of non-governmental entities, both in the violation and the support of human rights is receiving increasing attention. To the victims it does not make much difference, whether their human rights are violated by government forces or by irregular guerrilleas. On the other hand, non-governments actors, such as multilaterals or other major corporations, may be of great relevance. Some corporations – partly urged on by non-governmental human rights organizations – are gradually coming to realize that it is no longer sufficient 'to obey the law of the land', but that they have a responsibility of their own in contributing to the maintenance of human rights standards.

Victims of human rights violations that survive, often end up as political refugees and asylum seekers. Their plight in the host countries may be better than in the places they escaped from, but it is often far from satisfactory, to put it mildly. Western governments show themselves increasingly reluctant to accept such refugees, often because of an unreasonable fear of what the Germans almost untranslatably call *Ueberfremdung* ('overforeignization'). Nevertheless, governments that claim human rights as a cornerstone of their foreign policy, should realize that care for political refugees is part and parcel of such a policy.

A positive development is the increasing international attention that is being paid to violations of the human rights of women, including such violations that take place in the privacy of the home. Women's organizations have been rather successful in their efforts to bring such matters to public attention.

The human rights situation in the world is still far from perfect. It should be everybody's responsibility to make an effort to improve the situation. In Mary Robinson memorable words: 'We are all the custodians of human rights.' This book is meant to provide material for such activities.

This edition of *Human Rights: Universality in Practice* has been marginally revised and brought up to date to the year 2000. The section about the European Convention on Human Rights reflects the coming into force of the Eleventh Protocol. A few bibliographical references have been added.

PETER R. BAEHR
Heemstede, the Netherlands

Preface

This book is the result of many years of study and active involvement in human rights. The fiftieth anniversary of the Universal Declaration of Human Rights formed the direct occasion for its publication. The question of to what extent human rights are universal is the general overall theme of the book. It is explicitly dealt with in a number of places.

In the course of time, human rights have increasingly become an important subject of international politics. In this book an effort is made to emphasize the political aspects of human rights, without ignoring their legal nature. Chapters 3, 4, 5, 9, 10 and 11 are entirely new; chapters 1, 2, 6, 7 and 8 are based on texts that have appeared in my earlier book *The Role of Human Rights in Foreign Policy* (2nd edn, 1996). A Dutch version of this book was published in Amsterdam.

I am most grateful to my colleagues at the Netherlands Institute of Human Rights (SIM) and the School of Human Rights Research for creating the stimulating environment in which this book was being written. I thank my students in Leiden and Utrecht for their interest and their critical questions which have greatly inspired me. Experiences within Amnesty International taught me a great deal about the crucial importance of non-governmental organizations in the promotion of human rights.

I want to thank more in particular Saskia Bal and Mignon Senders for indispensable research assistance, and Kitty Arambulo, Ineke Boerefijn, and Brigit Toebes for their helpful comments. The full responsibility for the use of the commentary and the source material rests of course solely with the author.

PETER R. BAEHR
Heemstede/Utrecht

1 Introduction

THE MEANING OF HUMAN RIGHTS

Much lip-service is paid nowadays to the notion of human rights. At the same time, these human rights are being violated all over the world. Human rights are a matter of law, but they have increasingly become a matter of politics as well. Lawyers, politicians and governments, non-governmental organizations, men and women, the elderly as well as children, violators as well as victims – all of them are involved in human rights. What, then, are human rights?

Human rights are internationally agreed values, standards or rules regulating the conduct of states towards their own citizens and towards non-citizens. Human rights are, in the words of the preamble of the Universal Declaration of Human Rights: 'a common standard of achievement for all peoples and all nations'. These rules, which states have imposed upon themselves, serve to restrict the freedom of states to act towards their entire population: citizens as well as non-citizens, men as well as women, adults as well as children, whites and non-whites, believers and non-believers, married persons and the unmarried, heterosexuals as well as homosexuals. This situation is different from the past, when states, or rather their princes, were absolute sovereigns who could treat their subjects in any way they wanted. Nowadays, human beings have rights: *human rights*.

Human rights tell states what they may not do (state abstention), but also what they are supposed to do (state obligations). These prohibitions and obligations are strongly interrelated. For example, states may not summarily or arbitrarily arrest people or put them to death, they may not torture people, they may not deny them freedom of expression and freedom of association and peaceful assembly. On the other hand, they must care for fair trials, for the equal protection of the law, for a minimum standard of living, including food, clothing, housing, medical care and education.

Human rights are not absolute. A process of weighing out is necessary (for example by an independent court), if different rights come into conflict with each other. For example, freedom of expression is liable to a number of restrictions. It is not allowed, in the words of the nineteenth-century United States Supreme Justice Oliver Wendell Holmes 'to cry fire in a crowded theatre' (at least if there is no such fire). But also 'any advocacy of national, racial or religious hatred that constitutes incitement to discrimination, hostility or violence' shall be prohibited by law.[1] In Germany and France, the denial of the Holocaust is prohibited by law.[2] But there are also certain rules with regard to this type of prohibition. The call of the late Iranian spiritual leader, the Ayatollah Khomeini, to execute the author Salman Rushdie, who allegedly had been guilty of blasphemy against the Prophet Mohammed, is a violation of such rules.[3]

Views about the contents of human rights may change over time. In ancient Athens the confession or testimony of a slave was only accepted if he had been subjected to torture. After all, what reason would a slave have to confess or to betray his master, if he had not been tortured? In the Middle Ages, torture was considered as the *probatio probatissima*, the 'proof of all proofs'. Nowadays, views have entirely changed and torture is seen as a degrading and unacceptable violation of human dignity. Confessions obtained by torture or in any illegal manner are explicitly *not* accepted as proof. A person who is tortured, may 'confess' to all kinds of things, if only to be released from pain.[4]

BASIC DOCUMENTS

The two most important historic human rights documents are of western origin: the Virginia Bill of Rights of 1776 which was incorporated in 1791 in the United States Constitution, and the French Declaration of the Rights of Man and Citizen of 1789. Both documents contain a list of human rights in the sense of individual liberties. Many of these rights are based on the writings of political philosophers such as John Locke, Montesquieu and Jean-Jacques Rousseau.[5]

The preamble of the Charter of the United Nations explicitly mentions the notion of fundamental human rights. Article 1, paragraph 3 states as one of the purposes of the United Nations the achievement of 'international cooperation in solving international problems of an economic, social, cultural, or humanitarian character, and in promoting and encouraging respect for human rights and for fundamental freedoms for all without distinction as to race, sex, language or religion'. This led in 1948 to the adoption by the General Assembly of the Universal Declaration of Human Rights (see Appendix).

Human rights were incorporated in these UN documents as a reaction to the outrageous crimes against humanity committed by the National Socialists in Germany between 1933 and 1945. The torture and killing of more than six million Jews, gypsies, homosexuals and political opponents was the largest-scale violation of fundamental human rights in modern times. Concepts such as 'genocide' and 'crimes against humanity' are inseparably linked to this period in world history.

The Universal Declaration contains a list of the most important human rights. These include the following civil and political rights:

- the right to life, liberty and security of person (Article 3);
- the prohibition of slavery (Article 4);
- the prohibition of torture (Article 5);
- the prohibition of arbitrary arrest, detention or exile (Article 9);
- the right to a fair trial (Article 10);
- the right to freedom of movement (Article 13);
- the right to property (Article 17);
- the right to freedom of thought, conscience and religion (Article 18);
- the right to freedom of opinion and expression (Article 19);
- the right to freedom of assembly and association (Article 20);
- the right to participate in the government of one's country (Article 21).

The Universal Declaration also mentions some important social and economic rights:

- the right to work (Article 23);
- the right to an adequate standard of living, including food, clothing, housing and medical care (Article 25);
- the right to education (Article 26).

Cultural rights include the right to participate in the cultural life of one's community, to share in scientific advancement and the right to the protection of the moral and material interests resulting from one's scientific, literary or artistic production (Article 27).

These rights have been elaborated in two legally binding international treaties which were adopted by the General Assembly in 1966: the International Covenant on Civil and Political Rights and the International Covenant on Economic, Social and Cultural Rights. They differ from the Universal Declaration in that they do not include the right to seek asylum, the right to nationality and the right to property. The Covenant on Civil and Political Rights adds to the Universal Declaration that all persons deprived of their liberty shall be treated with humanity and with respect for the inherent dignity of the human person and that no one shall be liable to be tried or punished again for an offence for which he has already been finally convicted or acquitted. Both covenants mention explicitly in Article 1 the right of all peoples to self-determination. The covenants are more detailed than the Universal Declaration and contain a number of specific restrictions. Both entered into force in 1976. The Covenant on Civil and Political Rights has now (2000) been ratified by 147 States, the Covenant on Economic, Social and Cultural Rights by 142 States.

The Universal Declaration of Human Rights was adopted by the UN General Assembly as a resolution. Such resolutions have the legal status of recommendation, which means that they are not legally binding. However, it is by now commonly accepted that the so-called 'core rights' in the Universal Declaration have acquired the status of (binding) international customary law.[6]

Core rights are rights that are indispensable for an existence in human dignity and therefore need absolute protection. They include the right to life and the right to the inviolability of the human person, including the prohibition of slavery, serfdom, and torture, wrongful detention, discrimination and other acts that violate human dignity. In addition, the right to freedom of religion is often mentioned in this list.[7] In a recent article, two Dutch legal scholars go even further. Twenty-four treaties concluded by the European Communities and third states contain articles that explicitly stipulate the respect for human rights that are mentioned in the Universal Declaration. From this, the authors conclude, at least for the EC and its member-states, the *entire* Universal Declaration should be considered as binding.[8]

Bodies of the United Nations have repeatedly confirmed the importance of the Universal Declaration. Many declarations and resolutions call on states to respect the standards set out in the Universal Declaration. In 1968, the first World Conference on Human Rights adopted the Proclamation of Teheran, in which the Universal Declaration was proclaimed as stating a common understanding of the peoples of the world concerning the inalienable and inviolable rights of all members of the human family and constituting an obligation for the members of the international community. In the Final Declaration of the second World Conference on Human Rights, which was held in Vienna in 1993, the Universal Declaration was named the source of inspiration and the basis for the United Nations in making advances in standard-setting as contained in the existing international human rights instruments. Increasingly, the Universal Declaration, or at least certain parts of it, are considered to be part of international customary law.[9]

HIERARCHY OF HUMAN RIGHTS

It is not common practice to put human rights in any hierarchical order. At the United Nations it is frowned upon to say that certain human rights are more important than others. Nevertheless, there clearly exists some difference among them. Thus there are rights which, according to article 4 of the International Covenant on Civil and Political Rights, may not be derogated from, even in a state of public emergency. Such rights include the protection of the right to life, the prohibition of torture, the prohibition of slavery and the freedom of thought, conscience and religion, but none of the social and economic rights. However, other human rights treaties name other rights as 'non-derogable'.

In this context it should be mentioned that international experts, meeting in Syracuse, Italy in 1984, have tried to further define the conditions and grounds for permissible limitations and derogations of human rights. The point of departure was that such conditions and grounds should themselves be clearly defined and strongly limited.[10] So far, these proposals have not been put in an international, legally binding treaty.

GOVERNMENT ABSTENTION

The fundamental rights and freedoms emphasize the need for *government abstention* with regard to the rights of the individual. A government is not allowed to torture and should not allow its servants to do so. It may not interfere in the right of people to associate and to assemble freely; it may not interfere in the freedom of the press and freedom of expression.

But that is not the whole story. Sometimes, a government must do something in order to guarantee that the rights and freedoms can actually be exercised. For example, the right to a fair trial can only be realized if there are sufficient trained lawyers to conduct such trials and if the judicial authorities have the necessary technical means at their disposal. Sometimes, the freedom of assembly can only be exercised under police protection against political opponents. The right to participate in the government of one's country, 'directly or through freely chosen representatives' (Universal Declaration of Human Rights, Article 21) requires the organization of free and secret elections by the government. Training facilities, libraries and other provisions will normally be supplied by the government. Full government abstention is, in other words, not enough to guarantee respect for these rights and liberties. The opposite may be true.

In the case of social and economic rights, the need for government intervention is even greater. The realization of such rights as the right to work, the right to education, the right to medical care and the right to social security is nowadays unthinkable without some measure of government involvement. There may be political differences of view about the extent of this government involvement, but the nineteenth-century idea of the 'night-watchman state' has been abandoned.

THREE 'GENERATIONS' OF HUMAN RIGHTS

Human rights literature usually makes a distinction among three 'generations' of human rights.[11] The first generation refers to civil and political rights – the 'classic' human rights. Economic, social and cultural rights belong to the second generation. The third generation consists of collective rights which have received increasing attention in recent years.[12] Such rights are the following:

- the right to development, which, however, is also seen as a right of individuals;
- the right to peace;
- the right to a clean natural environment;
- the right to one's own natural resources;
- the right to one's own cultural heritage.

The latter two rights are usually considered to be part of the common heritage of mankind. Some of these third-generation rights, which have been mainly emphasized by the former communist and the Third World states, are rather controversial in the eyes of the West. They have been criticized for their vagueness and lack of clarity. Take, for example, the right to peace, which used to be strongly emphasized by the Soviet Union;[13] most people will be in favour of an abstract notion of peace, but that notion only acquires real meaning when answers are given to such questions as: peace under what circumstances and at what price? It is moreover unclear who could exercise such a right to peace – individuals, groups or states – and how it can be enforced. On the other hand, Katarina Tomaševski has a point when she argues that the conception of peace as a human right might help in 'raising public awareness that everyone has a stake in peace-keeping, widening public support for disarmament policy'.[14]

The term 'generations' is somewhat unfortunate. It suggests a succession of phenomena, whereby a new generation takes the place of the previous one. That is, however, not the case with the three 'generations' of human rights. On the contrary. The idea is rather that the three 'generations' exist and be respected simultaneously. Moreover, there is the curious phenomenon that one particular right – that of self-determination – belongs both to the first and the second 'generations'. It is mentioned in the International Covenant on Civil and Political Rights and in the International Covenant on Economic, Social and Cultural Rights. The reason is that the African and Asian states, which already were in the majority when the two treaties were adopted by the General Assembly in 1966, wanted in this way to emphasize the importance of this right.[15] It is a peoples' right that thus also belongs to the third generation of human rights. The word 'generations' should have been replaced by 'categories'.[16]

IMPORTANCE OF HUMAN RIGHTS

The international standards called 'human rights' are laid down in many legally binding treaties as well as in non-binding declarations. The Universal Declaration of Human Rights and the two human rights covenants of 1966 are commonly referred to as the 'international bill of human rights'. Next to these, there are many other declarations and treaties which will be dealt with in subsequent chapters.

At the same time, one must note on the basis of the reports of the United Nations themselves, of Amnesty International and other human rights organizations, that the international standards are often being violated. What is the purpose of the operation, one may be tempted to ask oneself? Why establish a long list of rights, which are continuously being violated all over the world? The answer is simple and can be found by referring to the situation in the national context. National criminal and penal laws are as often violated as international human rights standards. However, that is no reason to abolish such national laws. Similarly in international society there is no reason to abolish international human rights standards. Crimes such as murder, theft and rape are in most national societies prohibited. Nevertheless, they do occur all the time. Should the penal laws prohibiting them therefore be abolished? No, on the contrary: they must not be abolished, but the supervision of the laws should be improved. The same reasoning applies to international society. International standards are not found in laws, but in declarations and binding treaties. Similar to the national context but worse, international supervision is woefully inadequate. In an ideal world, laws and treaties in the field of human rights would be superfluous. In a world that is far from perfect, there is a great need for such instruments. They will be looked at in subsequent chapters.

2 Universalism versus Cultural Relativism

INTRODUCTION

Universal human rights instruments are based on the assumption that they reflect universally accepted norms of behaviour. This is important, among other things, for the role of the United Nations in supervising the observation of these international standards. Unless human rights – or at least a nucleus of such rights – are universally accepted, the United Nations will lack the basis on which its supervision activities are founded.

That assumption governed the approval in 1948 of the Universal Declaration of Human Rights by the General Assembly of the United Nations. It states in the beginning of its preamble that the 'recognition of the inherent dignity and of the equal and inalienable rights of all members of the human family is the foundation of freedom, justice and peace in the world'. That is also the foundation of the two international covenants on human rights, which were adopted in 1966.

No member-state of the United Nations voted in 1948 against adoption of the Universal Declaration of Human Rights. Eight states – the Soviet Union and five of its allies, plus Saudi Arabia and South Africa – abstained. One of the reasons why the Soviet Union abstained was that it felt that the Universal Declaration paid too little attention to the importance of the maintenance of national sovereignty. Soviet delegate Andrej Vishinskij rejected the notion that there existed rights of the individual beyond the context of the state.[1] The Soviet Union also held views of its own with regard to the issue of freedom of opinion, which should, for instance, not include the expression of fascist or racist views.[2] Saudi Arabia's abstention was based on its rejection of the inclusion under freedom of religion the right of *changing* one's religion. The latter is not permitted to a religious Muslim. South Africa rejected the principle of equality, laid down in Articles 1 and 2 of the Declaration.

However, the acceptance of these texts does not mean that the universal nature of human rights is a foregone conclusion. Among often-heard criticisms of the Universal Declaration are the following:[3]

- it was drafted at a time when most Third World nations were still under colonial domination; developing nations that later incorporated

9

the standards of the Universal Declaration in their national constitutions or accepted them as members of the Organization of American States or the Organization of African Unity, did so under
western pressure;[4]

- furthermore, the rights contained in the Universal Declaration are
  said to reflect mainly western ideological views, rather than values
  dominant in non-western societies;[5]
- the Declaration uses an individualistic approach to human rights,
  which is supposedly not suitable for societies that emphasize collective values.

In the eyes of a superficial observer, the question of the universality of
human rights seemed to be resolved at the World Conference of
Human Rights held in Vienna in 1993. In the Final Declaration of that
Conference it was stated: 'All human rights are universal, indivisible
and interdependent and interrelated.'[6] However, this was followed by
the ominous addition, that has since then been quoted on many occasions, that 'the significance of national and regional particularities and
various historical, cultural and religious backgrounds must be borne in
mind'.[7] The precise meaning of this addition, which was obviously the
result of a political compromise, has remained unclear. Yet, it is precisely the scope and meaning of these 'regional particularities' that are
at stake, if one raises the question of the universality of human rights.

It is clear that all governments apparently consider it important at
least to pay lip-service to the universal character of human rights. This
includes the governments of countries such as Indonesia, China, Singapore and Malaysia that are often cited as being critical of the notion of
the universal nature of human rights. Their ministers of foreign affairs
made a point of stating at the World Conference that human rights
were 'of course' universal in nature. The preamble of the Bangkok
Declaration, which was the result of a regional conference in preparation of the World Conference in which most Asian states participated,
stated explicitly: '*Stressing* the universality, objectivity and non-selectivity
of all human rights and the need to avoid the application of double
standards in the implementation of human rights and its politicization.'
It would not be difficult to supplement this example with similar
declarations by representatives of the other geographical regions of
the world. There can be little doubt that the concept of human rights
is seen as something very positive the world over, the universality
of which is not being denied. That leaves open the meaning which is
being attached to it.

There is a big difference between universalism in standard-setting and universalism in implementation. With regard to the latter there can be little doubt: there is none. Consultation of the annual reports of Amnesty International and other human rights organizations, but also of organs of the United Nations and the United States Department of State, demonstrate that there is no universal respect for human rights. That is hardly surprising. If there existed universal implementation of human rights, it would hardly be necessary to codify them in international treaties and to design complex supervisory mechanisms.

In determining the universal character of human rights various criteria can be applied. A very strong criterion would be, for example, that all human beings all over the world should agree about the meaning of human rights as well as about its implementation. Obviously, such a criterion cannot be met for the time being. Not all human beings share the same view about the meaning of human rights and there exists no agreement about the mutual relationship of various human rights. Should one want to apply such a criterion, then the conclusion would likely be that there is no such universalism of human rights.

A weaker criterion would be that political elites all over the world should agree on the meaning of human rights. This demand would be hard to fulfil, too. Political elites seem to differ in particular on the precise nature and meaning of human rights. There appears to be a great difference between the pronouncements made at the World Conference on Human Rights in 1993 in Vienna by the ministers of Foreign Affairs of a number of Asian states and those of western ministers.[8]

At the level of non-governmental organizations, the universalism of human rights has indeed been 'universally' accepted. The conference of Asian governments in Bangkok (29 March until 2 April 1993) was preceded by a meeting of Asian non-governmental organizations (25–28 March 1993). That meeting resulted in a (non-governmental) Bangkok Declaration on Human Rights, which left no doubt about the universal character of these rights:

> Universal human rights standards are rooted in many cultures. We affirm the basis of universality of human rights which afford protection to all of humanity, including special groups such as women, children, minorities and indigenous peoples, workers, refugees and displaced persons, the disabled and the elderly. *While advocating cultural pluralism, those cultural practices which derogate from universally accepted human rights including women's rights, must not be tolerated* [italics supplied]. **As human rights are of universal concern and are**

> **universal in value, the advocacy of human rights cannot be considered to be an encroachment upon national sovereignty.**[9]

These non-governmental organizations did not hide behind a notion of cultural relativism, defending violations of international human rights standards with an appeal to alleged 'other' culturally determined values.[10] On the contrary, they demanded that where cultural practices deviate from international human rights standards, the latter ought to prevail.

Although, at a rather high abstract level, NGOs accept the universalism of human rights, this does not mean that inside such organizations there exists always agreement about their significance. A well-known example is the debate which lasted for many years among members of Amnesty International, on the question whether the organization should work for the release of persons who had been imprisoned because of their homosexuality. Amnesty sections in western countries were strongly in favour, while many Asian, African and Latin-American sections thought differently. There, homosexuality was seen as an illness or deviation, having nothing to do with human rights. In their view, it would be ridiculous if Amnesty were to work for the release of homosexual detainees and risk becoming involved in having to rule on all kinds of other sexual practices. The difference of view, which culminated in a debate about the 'mandate' of the organization, was finally decided in favour of working for the release of such detained persons.[11] The question whether this decision has harmed the development of the organization in Third World countries, as the opponents claimed, remains difficult to answer.[12]

DIFFERENCES OF VIEW

The desire to protect the rights of the individual belongs to the best western traditions which relate human rights primarily to rights of individuals which should not be violated by any other individual, group or authority. Here lies a crucial difference with dominant non-western approaches. Jack Donnelly has made the point that the emphasis on the individual is one of the most important differences between modern western and non-western views of human dignity.[13] He has argued that the protection of the individual against the demands of society was originally not part of traditional non-western thinking.

Mr Ali Alatas, the Foreign Minister of Indonesia, argued at the second World Conference on Human Rights in Vienna for the need of finding a balance between the rights of the individual and the rights of the community: 'Indonesian culture as well as its ancient well-developed customary laws have traditionally put high priority on the rights and interests of the society or nation, without however in any way minimizing or ignoring the rights and interests of individuals and groups.'[14] However, even if one accepts Mr Alatas' argument, an unsolved point of discussion remains: which person or group in authority is going to interpret those rights of society? How is it to be guaranteed that the true rights of society are taken into account? That question is obviously more a matter of implementation than of acceptance of human rights standards. Under traditional international law, on the whole the claim of governments that they are the legitimate representatives of the people they govern is accepted. However, individual persons may gain by standing on their own in international law, as is the case under the European Convention of Human Rights and Fundamental Freedoms and the (first) Optional Protocol to the International Covenant on Civil and Political Rights, which recognize the right of individual complaint. Proposals to establish a similar right under the International Covenant on Economic, Social and Cultural Rights are receiving close attention in governmental as well as non-governmental circles.[15]

If one accepts Donnelly's view of the difference between western and non-western conceptions of human rights, this does not necessarily mean that in modern times no truly 'universal' norms have been developed. It is at least conceivable that conceptions of human rights, which were originally western, have been accepted or will be accepted by non-western societies, and vice versa. The fact that the protection of individual rights is based on western ideas does not exclude such ideas being adopted by others and being developed into norms that have universal validity. By way of analogy it can be argued that the roots of international communism lie in the West and were first developed by western thinkers (both Karl Marx and Friedrich Engels were born and grew up in Germany). Yet, at present the most important remaining manifestations of communist thinking, except for Fidel Castro's Cuba, are to be found not in western countries but in Asia: the People's Republic of China, the Democratic People's Republic of Korea, the Lao People's Democratic Republic and Viet Nam.

There are indications that at least certain human rights have gained universal acceptance. Almost all governments, whatever their ideological or cultural background, condemn systematic and gross violations of human rights, such as genocide, torture or involuntary disappearances. But not only is there a growing interest among non-western actors in individual rights, the idea of collective rights is increasingly being accepted in the West as well as in the East. That is not only true for the right of self-determination, which is listed prominently in the two international human rights covenants of 1966 (Article 1). It is also true for the rights of indigenous people(s) which receive increasing attention in western countries as well.[16] It is also increasingly being suggested that rights of (ethnic, religious, racial and linguistic) minorities should be recognized, next to those of *members* of such minorities (as mentioned in Article 27 of the International Covenant on Civil and Political Rights). The very denial of rights to such minorities in countries such as the former Yugoslavia and Rwanda, has led to louder calls for guaranteeing their rights in international instruments. This is less surprising than may appear at first sight: we should remember that it was in great part due to the Nazi atrocities against the Jews, gypsies, homosexuals and political opponents that led to the renewed call for the formulation of human rights, as they were enshrined in 1948 in the Universal Declaration of Human Rights.

Since 1948, the principles of the Universal Declaration have been repeatedly reaffirmed in international gatherings, such as the world conferences on human rights held in Teheran in 1968 and in Vienna in 1993. Governments have not distanced themselves from the Declaration. The declaration adopted at the Vienna Conference states explicitly: 'The universal nature of these rights and freedoms is beyond question.'[17] It is, moreover, not left exclusively to individual governments to take care of the promotion and protection of human rights. No, this is 'a legitimate concern of the international community'.[18]

However, not all governments that participated in the Vienna Conference seem to have fully accepted that message. The Indonesian Foreign Minister, Mr Alatas, expressed himself as follows:

> While human rights are indeed universal in character, it is now generally acknowledged that their expression and implementation in the national context should remain the competence and responsibility of each government. This means that the complex variety of problems, of different economic, social and cultural realities, and the unique value systems prevailing in each country should be taken into consideration. This national competence not only derives from the principle of sovereignty of states, but also is a logical consequence of the principle of self-determination.[19]

That is true up to a point. The 147 states that have ratified the International Covenant on Civil and Political Rights have undertaken to submit reports to the United Nations on the measures they have adopted to give effect to the rights recognized therein and on the progress made in the enjoyment of those rights (ICCPR, Article 40). These reports are submitted to the UN Committee on Human Rights whose 18 independent expert members study those reports and express their views on them. A similar procedure exists under the International Covenant on Economic, Social and Cultural Rights, which by now has been ratified by 142 states (ICESCR, Article 16). In other words, for those states that have ratified these treaties, their governments' views on human rights performance in their countries are not the final word. This excludes of course the 60-odd nations, including Indonesia, that have not yet ratified the two covenants. In other words, what Mr Alatas had to say was perhaps true for his own country, but not for the majority of the states of the world.

The Dutch human rights expert Pieter van Dijk has rightly observed that, if countries like China and Indonesia object to being judged by western states with allegedly western points of view, they should subject themselves to supervision by the independent Human Rights Committee: 'The findings of that Committee, based on the submitted periodic reports and possible individual complaints, could supply these States with a defence against the Western countries, in so far as these findings would be positive to their case.'[20]

The quoted statement of the Indonesian minister may be valid for his own country, but not for the majority of states in the world. It is remarkable that the preamble of the Bangkok Declaration of the Regional Meeting for Asia preparatory to the World Conference on Human Rights which met in Bangkok (29 March–2 April 1993), in which most Asian states participated, emphasizes that ratification of international human rights instruments, *particularly the International Covenant on Civil and Political Rights and the International Covenant on Economic, Social and Cultural Rights* [italics supplied], should be further encouraged. However, 13 of the Asian states that participated in the Conference have not done so thus far.[21]

FOOD OR FREEDOM

The often-heard view that certain human rights are not (or not yet) applicable to non-western societies, is in fact a reflection of a rather paternalistic way of thinking: 'Freedom of expression may be important to westerners, but people in the developing world have not yet reached that stage.' Thus it is often said that developing nations should first provide for basic commodities, such as food and medicine. As long as these basic means are not sufficiently available, it is supposedly not necessary to guarantee respect for civil and political rights. Especially repressive regimes often argue that there is no need for the protection of fundamental civil and political rights in their countries, as long as the population is undernourished and the country economically underdeveloped. They emphasize instead the development of economic and social rights.

There is, however, some justified ground for suspicion, if such arguments are put forward by governments. It has never been demonstrated that a restriction of civil and political rights does contribute to the economic development of a country. The only objective it may contribute to is the maintenance of the repressive regime itself! Also the victims of repression rarely argue for the right of their government to repress them. On the contrary, seen from the perspective of actual or potential victims, the acceptance of universal human rights seems to be much more universal than some governments claim. Moreover, the two UN covenants on human rights impose different obligations on the states parties. The respect for civil and political rights is not made dependent on the degree of economic development of a state. In most cases, there does not exist a logical connection between the recognition of certain civil and political rights on the one hand, and the degree of economic development on the other. There is no reason why, for example, the right not to be tortured should not equally apply to persons living in rich as well as in poor countries.

The ambassador of Singapore implicitly suggested at the World Conference on Human Rights that first poverty should be alleviated before people could be allowed to be free: 'Only those who have forgotten the pangs of hunger will think of consoling the hungry by telling them that they should be free before they can eat.'[22] No indeed! In line with the final statement of the conference, *both* rights should be realized, not one at the expense of the other. [To add a personal note: having myself survived a period of famine, when 20 000 people died of hunger in the German-occupied part of the Netherlands in the winter of 1945, it has occurred to me that the denial of food may be the direct consequence of the denial of freedom. For several months, the German occupation forces did not allow food to reach the hungry population.]

RIGHTS OR DUTIES

There is no doubt that the concept of human rights is interpreted differently according to its political and cultural context. In the past, a distinction was made between the 'East' and the 'West', meaning the communist as opposed to western-democratic states. Since the demise of communism in Eastern Europe, there remains a major division between the 'South' and the 'North', which refers to the distinction between the poor, underdeveloped,[23] mainly Asian and African states, and the industrialized West European and North American states.

The differences between East and West used to be in the emphasis they put on the rights of society as a whole versus individual rights, on economic and social rights versus civil and political rights, and on the protection of national sovereignty versus a strengthening of international supervision. The differences between the South and the North relate mainly to the importance that is attached to the right of self-determination, peoples' rights in general and the emphasis that is put, for example in the African Charter on Human Rights and Peoples' Rights, on *duties* toward society next to individual rights.

In the autumn of 1997, an international group of former government leaders, calling itself 'Inter Action Council', published a proposal to establish a Universal Declaration of International Responsibilities.[24] The General Assembly of the United Nations was supposed to adopt that declaration at the occasion of the fiftieth anniversary of the Universal Declaration of Human Rights. The draft declaration consists of a preamble and 19 articles. The proposal was presented by way of response to the present profound changes in the world as a result of the process of globalization. Global problems demand global solutions on the basis of ideas, values and norms respected by all cultures and societies. Rights and responsibilities should be given equal importance to establish an ethical base so that all men and women can live peacefully together and fufil their potential. Human aspirations for progress can only be realized by agreed values and standards applying to all people and all institutions at all times. The draft declaration seeks to bring freedom and responsibility into balance and to promote a move from the freedom of indifference to the freedom of involvement. It pays attention to fundamental principles of humanity, non-violence and respect for life, justice and solidarity, truthfulness and tolerance, mutual respect and partnership.

The said draft declaration contains a great number of principles that are worthy of consideration, but it is at the same time a threat to the universalism of human rights. As the Dutch human rights expert, Theo van Boven, has pointed out, '[B]y choosing the Universal Declaration of Human Rights as the frame of reference the impression is created, unintentionally, that the Universal Declaration of 1948 contributed to excesses of unbridled emphasis on human rights and freedoms.'[25] He considers the text as 'regrettably deficient' where it fails to point to the economic and financial actors which in the process of the globalization of the economy have become increasingly powerful and which should carry their due and proportional share when responsibilities and duties in the area of human rights are at stake.

The said differences are not static in nature, but evolve over time. Thus, views about human rights have changed from Stalin's reign over the Soviet Union to that of Gorbachev, Yeltsin and Putin over present-day Russia. In western countries views about certain economic and social rights are by no means static. Also, the various 'camps' are not monolithic. Within each 'camp' there are differences of view and interpretation over the importance to be accorded to certain specific human rights.

In its preamble, the Universal Declaration of Human Rights is proclaimed as a 'common standard of achievement'. It assumes the universality of norms on which that common standard should be based. There does not yet exist full agreement on the nature of those norms, but perhaps it is correct to speak, as the late John Vincent did, of an 'emerging consensus'.[26] Further evidence for this view may be found in the fact, as Antonio Cassese has pointed out, that newly adopted 'non-western' human rights documents, such as the African Charter on Human Rights and Peoples' Rights and the two Islamic Declarations on Human Rights, all reaffirm traditional human rights values.[27] The 'emerging consensus' provides an opportunity for a debate on the manner in which the norms that are contained in international declarations and conventions can best be implemented. Such a debate and the consensus that, it is hoped, may emerge from that debate, are indispensable conditions for arriving at a greater respect for human rights in all parts of the world.

CONCLUSION

Whatever the nature of cultural differences may be, universal acceptance of international human rights standards is not to be excluded. The reason is that just about all governments like to be seen as civilized and decent. They insist on defending their policies and ask for international understanding. That is also the reason why non-governmental organizations can use the instrument of the 'mobilization of shame' with a certain measure of effectiveness.[28] They base themselves on standards that are internationally accepted and report on violations of such standards. Governments do not like to be seen as violating human rights, even if they do so with an appeal to allegedly different cultural values. This opens the possibility for an international discussion about the way in which the values on which international declarations and treaties are based can be applied in practice. Such discussions may lead to an international consensus, which is an indispensable precondition for greater respect for human rights in the world. In the words of the intergovernmental Declaration of Bangkok: 'The respect and promotion of human rights should be encouraged by cooperation and consensus and not through confrontation and the imposition of incompatible values.'[29] Not so very long ago, slavery and torture were fully accepted in most societies. Nowadays, both are considered as violations of human rights and universally prohibited. The prohibition of racial discrimination seems to be moving in the same direction. Thus reaching such consensus is not a completely hopeless endeavour.

In order to avoid possible misunderstandings, it should be pointed out once again that this chapter has dealt with the acceptance of standards, not with the implementation of such standards. The fact that human rights are being violated all over the world is not an argument against universalism of standards. It only tells us something about deficiencies in overseeing those standards. Within national societies there are also such values and norms, laid down in national legislation. In all national societies murder and theft are prohibited. The fact that they do occur all the same, is not an argument to doubt the value of such norms or to delete them from national legislation. The same is true of international standards: they are insufficiently respected, but that does not mean that no consensus can be reached about the nature of such standards.

3 Gross and Systematic Violations

INTRODUCTION

When human rights are mentioned, one usually thinks first of the classic civil and political rights. These are mentioned in the Universal Declaration of Human Rights, the International Covenant on Civil and Political Rights, and regional treaties such as the European Convention of Human Rights and Fundamental Freedoms, the American Convention on Human Rights, and the African Charter on Human Rights and Peoples' Rights. In this chapter, gross violations of such rights are examined.

The term 'gross, systematic violations' refers to violations, instrumental to the achievement of governmental policies, perpetrated in such a quantity and in such a manner as to create a situation in which the rights to life, to personal integrity or to personal liberty of the population as a whole or of one or more sectors of the population of a country are continuously infringed or threatened.[1]

The following violations are among the most important at issue: the prohibition of slavery, the right to life, torture and cruel, inhuman or degrading treatment or punishment, genocide, disappearances and 'ethnic cleansing'.[2]

SLAVERY

UN Secretary-General Kofi Annan recently spoke of the continued practice of slavery all over the world. Hundreds of thousands of people still live and die as slaves. Women and children are particularly vulnerable to all forms of slavery, including forced labour and prostitution, as well as the sale and exploitation of children.[3]

Slavery is forced labour, the result of which must be partly or fully ceded and whereby the worker is the physical property of the master.[4] Until about the middle of the nineteenth century, slavery was extensively practised and permitted. A great deal of money was earned in the trading of slaves, who were shipped under abominable circumstances from Africa to the American continent. There they were sold by auction. From the end of the eighteenth century voices began to be heard which condemned slavery as a violation of human dignity. In 1863, slavery was officially abolished in the United States, in 1880 in Brazil, and in some countries as late as the twentieth century.[5]

Internationally, slavery was prohibited by the League of Nations in the Slavery Convention of 1926. In 1953, a protocol was adopted which transferred the tasks of the League of Nations to the United Nations, and in 1956 a supplementary convention was adopted. The Convention forbids slave trade and aims at ending all forms of slavery. It is striking that only 79 states, i.e. less than half of the members of the United Nations, are parties to this Convention (1997). Such countries as China, Indonesia, Iran, Japan, Malaysia, Singapore, Thailand, Argentina, Colombia, and Peru are not parties to the Convention and/ or the Protocol.

Slavery is prohibited in all general human rights treaties.[6] In 1975, the UN Sub-Commission on Prevention of Discrimination and Protection of Minorities established a Working Group on Contemporary Forms of Slavery. These include, in addition to traditional slavery, traffic in persons, the sale of children, child prostitution, child pornography, the exploitation of child labour, the sexual mutilation of female children, the use of children in armed conflicts, debt bondage, traffic in the sale of human organs, the exploitation of prostitution, exploitation of migrant labour, and sex tourism.[7] The Working Group acts as a contact for non-governmental organizations with consultative status, the most important of which is the Anti-Slavery Society. The Working Group has been criticized for its lack of a clear focus and of effective procedures to give a follow-up to its conclusions and recommendations.[8] Other modern forms of slavery are the repression of women in general and traffic in women in particular.[9] This is prohibited in the Convention for the Suppression of the Traffic in Persons and of the Exploitation of the Prostitution of Others of 1949; this Convention, which entered into force in 1951, has been ratified by only 73 states (2000).

Slavery in all its forms is a gross violation of human rights. It is a denial of the equal dignity and equality of rights of all human beings. There are, however, major financial interests at stake, which makes it hard to fight slavery effectively. It is nevertheless of fundamental importance that slavery is brought to an end. There ought not to be a place for it in the modern age.

THE RIGHT TO LIFE

All general instruments on human rights include an article on the right to life.[10] This means at the very least that nobody should be arbitrarily put to death. That is why so-called extra-judicial executions are prohibited, although there is still a great deal of discussion on the precise meaning of that term.[11] Since 1982, a Special Rapporteur on Summary and Arbitrary Executions has submitted an annual report to the UN Commission on Human Rights.

In countries where the death penalty still exists,[12] it applies only to the most serious crimes and cannot be applied to pregnant women or minors. Even in countries that have abolished the death penalty, there remains always the possibility that it may be reintroduced under special circumstances such as war or if a wave of violent crimes occurs. According to its opponents,[13] the death penalty is an unacceptable violation of the right to life and of the right to be free from cruel, inhuman and degrading punishment. All kinds of cruel penalties, such as the rack, thumb-screws, or breaking on the wheel, have become prohibited over the centuries, on humanitarian grounds. Only the ultimate physical punishment – the death penalty – still exists. The death penalty is, moreover, the only punishment which cannot be undone; a sentence, which afterwards turns out have been pronounced on faulty grounds, cannot be corrected.[14]

There exists no international agreement about the meaning of the right to life for the maintenance of the death penalty. A large number of states, including the United States of America, have entered a reservation with regard to Article 6 of the International Covenant on Civil and Political Rights. Eighty-seven states retain the death penalty in their national legislation and actual practice; in 20 states, the death penalty still exists for ordinary crimes, but it has not been applied during the last ten years; in 13 states the death penalty exists only for exceptional crimes, such as crimes under military law or if committed under special circumstances such as war; in 75 states, the death penalty has been fully abolished.[15] According to data collected by Amnesty International, in 2000 at least, 1457 prisoners were executed in 28 countries and 3058 persons were sentenced to death in 65 countries.[16]

So far, only 43 states have ratified the Second Optional Protocol to the International Covenant on Civil and Political Rights, which prohibits the death penalty; the Sixth Protocol to the European Convention on Human Rights has been ratified by 39, and signed by three European states; the Protocol to the American Convention to Abolish the Death

Penalty has been ratified by seven, and signed by two American states (2000).

Differences about the acceptability of the death penalty are not limited to controversies between countries of the North and countries of the South. The United States of America is a country of the North where the death penalty continues to exist and it is applied in most American states.[17] Cyprus, and Israel are countries of the North that maintain the death penalty in time of war. The other countries of the North are among the 75 states which have fully abolished the death penalty.

Within all countries there exist profound differences of view about the precise meaning of the right to life. The question of when life begins continues to divide proponents and opponents of legalized abortion. Should the unborn child be protected by the right to life? Most international treaties are silent on this issue[18] and in most countries it is difficult to reach consensus on this subject. Also, with regard to euthanasia, public discussion in most countries is unresolved – or has not even started yet.[19]

TORTURE

Torture is prohibited everywhere.[20] The International Convention against Torture and Other Cruel, Inhuman or Degrading Treatment or Punishment has the following long as well as complicated definition of torture:

> any act by which severe pain or suffering, whether physical or mental, is intentionally inflicted on a person for such purposes as obtaining from him or a third person information or a confession, punishing him for an act he or a third person has committed or is suspected of having committed, or intimidating him or coercing him or a third person, or for any reason based on discrimination of any kind, when such pain or suffering is inflicted by or at the instigation of or with the consent or acquiescence of a public official or other person acting in an official capacity. It does not include pain or suffering arising only from, inherent in or incidental to lawful sanctions.[21]

This definition contains a number of important elements:

(1)   there must be an act that is intentional;
(2)   there must be strong physical or mental suffering;

(3)   the objective is to obtain information or a confession, to inflict a punishment or, more generally, to exercise intimidation;

(4)   there must be involvement by a public official; similar acts by private individuals are not considered as torture in the sense of the Treaty;

(5)   physical or mental punishment that are part of legal rules, are *not* considered as torture. The latter point has been rightly termed by Kooijmans 'an unfortunate product of a too large willingness to compromise'.[22] States, where physical punishment is still being practised, usually appeal to this formulation, if they are accused of condoning cruel, inhuman, or degrading punishment. Kooijmans has referred to pronouncements by the UN Human Rights Committee to the effect that the prohibition of cruel and inhuman punishment also includes corporal punishment.[23]

Torture has been termed a 'crime of obedience': an act performed in response to orders from authority that is considered illegal or immoral by the larger community.[24] Intent must be shown, when one has to decide whether or not a certain act is an act of torture. An unwitting infliction of pain is not considered as torture. The existence of torture schools where training in techniques of torture is provided, can be an indication of the existence of systematic torture.[25] The same is true of the availability of instruments of torture, though it is clear that simple objects, such as cigarettes, may be used for purposes of torture.

Next to the infliction of physical pain, there is the causing of mental suffering. Reference is made to 'sensoric deprivation' in cases of isolated confinement, a refined form of mental torture by totally cutting off all contacts of the prisoner with the world outside; all contrasts of light and sound are avoided, the sense of touch of the tortured person is eliminated. Prevention of sleep or putting a person in agonizing uncertainty about the his fate, belong to torture as a continued process of interrogation in a situation of increasing physical and mental exhaustion. It is a situation of permanent degradation, which may be even more intolerable than physical pain.

Torture is in the first place used as a means of intimidation and repression. Torture is applied to 'set an example', to break a person's resistance to an established position of power or to prevent such resistance from occurring, or even in order to strengthen a feeble power position. The most common justification of torture is, however, that it is necessary to obtain vital information, which cannot, or only too slowly, be acquired in any other way.[26] Well-known is the example of the arrested frogman who has put a timebomb to the hulk of a ship and who must be physically forced to tell the place of that bomb as otherwise the ship will explode. Is torture allowed under such circumstances? The answer is simple: no! Public officials or military officers who practise it nevertheless, must be put to trial afterwards and may appeal to mitigating circumstances.[27]

It is common to justify torture by referring to an alleged need for obtaining information, for example, for the army or the police. In addition, it is often said that such information may contribute to prevent worse things from happening, such as terrorist acts, which would put the lives of innocent persons at stake.[28] This manner of reasoning can be dealt with in two ways: (a) is torture an effective means for obtaining information? (b) if it is indeed effective, is it then permitted? To begin with the first question: there exists considerable doubt about the reliabilility of information that is obtained by torture. To what extent is information to be believed that is obtained by the application of physical or mental suffering? Is it not likely that a tortured person may 'confess' to anything if that means putting an end to his suffering? Other techniques, such as tapping conversations of prisoners or offering rewards, present useful alternatives to replace unreliable information obtained through torture. But even if torture resulted in reliable information, it is still to be rejected on moral-ethical grounds. Torture is a violation of the most fundamental concepts of human dignity and human integrity. It is a direct violation of human rights. Torture presupposes a fundamental inequality between the torturer and the tortured; the first denying the latter's very humanity. As far as there is still anything 'human' in the victim, it must be broken and he or she must be entirely subjected to the will of the torturer. When this has been achieved, once the free will of the victim is broken, he has lost some part of what makes him a complete human being – the power of independent thinking, of self-determination.

The supervision of the implementation of the prohibition of torture rests, according to the International Convention against Torture, with a committee of experts which studies the national reports of the states parties to the Convention. In addition, there is a Special UN Rapporteur who reports to the UN Commission on Human Rights. A proposal is now under discussion to add an Optional Protocol to the Convention which would create a sub-committee to the Committee on Torture, which would be authorized to visit places within the territory of the states parties where persons are being detained against their will. On the basis of these visits, the sub-committee would submit a confidential report to the state in question and enter into a dialogue with it about practical measures to improve the condition of the prisoners, with the ultimate aim of preventing torture.[29]

GENOCIDE

The term 'genocide' was coined in 1944 by the Polish jurist Raphael Lemkin.[30] He referred to the coordinated and planned elimination of a national, religious or racial group by activities directed to undermine the foundations of survival of the group in question. The immediate cause for formulating the term were the Nazi activities to eliminate the Jews.[31] Early in this century, the Turkish government had made a similar effort with reference to the Armenian people.[32] In the literature, for many years a discussion has been taking place about the precise definition of genocide and its difference from related concepts such as 'ethnocide' and 'politicide'.[33] Thus it has been suggested that the gas attacks by Iraqi military on the Kurds in Northern Iraq in 1987/88 should not be termed acts of genocide.[34]

In 1948, the General Assembly of the United Nations adopted the Convention on the Prevention and Punishment of the Crime of Genocide. Article II of the Convention describes genocide as any of the following acts committed with the intent to destroy, in whole or in part, a national, ethnic, racial or religious group, as such:

(a) Killing members of the group;
(b) Causing serious bodily or mental harm to members of the group;
(c) Deliberately inflicting on the group conditions of life calculated to bring about its physical destruction in whole or in part;
(d) Imposing measures intended to prevent births within the group;
(e) Forcibly transferring children of the group to another group.

Persons charged with genocide are to be tried by a competent tribunal of the state in the territory of which the act was committed, or by such international penal tribunal as may have jurisdiction (Article VI). This article has remained a dead letter, so far.[35] States parties to the Convention can submit disputes relating to the interpretation, application or fulfilment of the Convention to the International Court of Justice (Article IX). This has happened only once so far, when Bosnia-Herzegovina submitted a complaint against the Federal Republic of Yugoslavia (Serbia and Montenegro). This dispute is still under consideration. With regard to the mass killings by the Khmer Rouge in

Cambodia (1975–79), which resulted in the death of between one and two million people,[36] non-governmental organizations have urged governments to file a state complaint against Cambodia because of its violation of the Genocide Convention. The (non-governmental) Cambodia Documentation Commission in New York had collected extensive documentation material about genocide in Cambodia, on the basis of which it has urged states to arrive at an international condemnation of the crimes committed by the Khmer Rouge. However, no government has been willing to take such an initiative.

The United Nations has always been reluctant to employ the term 'genocide', as this might rule out negotiations with the government that has been so accused.[37] But in regard to the situation in the former Yugoslavia and in Rwanda the term 'genocide' has been used nevertheless. In the former Yugoslavia there were 'grave breaches and other violations of international humanitarian law (...) including willful killing, "ethnic cleansing",[38] mass killings, torture, rape, pillage and destruction of civilian property, destruction of cultural and religious property and arbitrary arrests'.[39] The killing of more than 6000 Muslims in the Bosnian enclave of Srebrenica has been termed by an independent observer 'Europe's worst massacre since the Second World War'.[40] In 1994, more than half a million Tutsis were cruelly killed by members of the Rwandan army, while more than one million Rwandese fled the country. This does not necessarily mean that all these misdeeds were acts of genocide,[41] but the Statute of the International Tribunal on the Former Yugoslavia explicitly mentions genocide as one of the crimes for which it may prosecute persons (Article 4). By way of definition, the terms of the Genocide Convention are used.[42] The same is true for the Rwanda Tribunal.[43]

In June 1996, the Yugoslavia Tribunal took up the cases of the Serbian-Bosnian leader Radovan Karadzic and General Ratko Mladic. Both were indicted for organizing a mass and systematic campaign of genocide and ethnic cleansing resulting in thousands of deaths.[44] The mandate of the Permanent International Criminal Court, which is the subject of a draft treaty adopted in the summer of 1998, includes acts of genocide.

The prohibition of genocide is a collective human right. Genocide can only be practised against groups of persons. There can be no doubt that the prohibition of genocide is of fundamental importance to human dignity. It is a human right to be free from elimination as a group. The Permanent Court will have the mandate to punish the culprits. It is, however, clear that neither the Genocide Convention nor the proposed Court will help to *prevent* genocide. Ways should be sought therefore to take preventive measures as well, such as setting up a databank with recent information about potential cases of genocide, commissioning studies about previous conflicts and developing a system of 'early warning'.[45] The crime of genocide is one of the most serious violations of the right to life. An effective fight against genocide has, however, only just begun.

DISAPPEARANCES[46]

In the 1960s and 1970s, in a number of Latin American countries a new form of gross and systematic violations of human rights manifested itself: the phenomenon of 'disappearances'.[47] Dissidents, opponents of the military regime in countries such as Guatemala, Argentina, Chile and Uruguay,[48] suddenly disappeared. When the concerned relatives asked the authorities for information, they were told that nothing was known about the case. Officials would suggest that the person in question had perhaps gone to visit his girlfriend, that he was in financial debt or had gone away for other reasons of a personal nature. As the cases usually concerned political opponents of the regime, the relatives did not easily accept such 'explanations' and continued to ask to be informed of the whereabouts of their beloved ones. Very often, it later turned out that the person in question had been put to death, often after having been tortured.

Starting in 1977, in Buenos Aires weekly public meetings took place of women, who were to be named the 'Mothers of the Plaza de Mayo'. Their objective was to shake their fellow-Argentinians from their apathy. They hoped in this way to find out what had happened to their children or other relatives.[49] The peaceful demonstrations of the 'Crazy Mothers' drew international attention and led to increasing pressure on the military regime. International non-governmental organizations also began to call attention to the disappearances. A Latin American Federation of Relatives of Disappeared Persons (FEDEFAM) was established, to coordinate the activities of the separate national organizations. The human rights organization Amnesty International started in 1980 a campaign against disappearances. Outside Latin America, citizens' committees were established for Chile, Argentina, Guatemala and other states, which pressured their own governments to do something about violations of human rights in Latin America in general and disappearances in particular.

According to the Declaration on the Protection of All Persons from Enforced Disappearance, which was adopted by the UN General Assembly in 1992,[50] disappearance constitutes a violation of the rules of international law guaranteeing, *inter alia*, the right to recognition as a person before the law, the right to liberty and security of the person and the right not to be subjected to torture and other cruel, inhuman or degrading treatment or punishment. Disappearance also violates or constitutes a grave threat to the right to life.[51] The Inter-American Convention on Forced Disappearances of Persons, which was adopted in 1994[52] defines disappearances as follows: '[T]he act of depriving a person or persons of his or their freedom, in whatever way, perpetrated by agents of the state or by persons or groups of persons acting with the authorization, support, or acquiescence of the state, followed by an absence of information or a refusal to acknowledge that deprivation of freedom or to give information on the whereabouts of that person, thereby impeding his or her recourse to the applicable legal remedies and procedural guaranties.'[53] The Inter-American Court of Human Rights in 1988 denounced disappearances as a 'flagrant denial of the values arising from the concept of human dignity'.[54]

Growing international concern led the UN Commission on Human Rights to establish a working group on Enforced or Involuntary Disappearances. This Working Group, which consists of five experts from the different geographical regions, reports annually on cases of disappearances all over the world. The Working Group is mandated to examine questions relating to the problem of enforced or involuntary disappearances. It employs five different techniques: routine requests for information, urgent action requests, country visits, prompt interventions, and reporting to the Commission on Human Rights.[55] During the first year of its existence, the Working Group received information about between 11 000 and 13 000 cases of disappearances.[56] In the year 2000, there were 49 070 unresolved cases of disappearances.[57] The Working Group expressed in particular concern over the following countries: Argentina, El Salvador, Guatemala, Peru, and Sri Lanka.[58] The Working Group urged states to invite it for a visiting mission. Of the newly reported cases, 120 allegedly occurred in 2000 in Algeria, Argentina, Colombia, Congo, India, Mexico, Morocco, Nepal, Pakistan, Russia, Rwanda, Sri Lanka, Tanzania, Ukraine, Uzbekistan, Yugoslavia, and Zimbabwe.[59]

There are, as was already indicated, two international instruments on disappearances: the United Nations Declaration on the Protection of All Persons from Enforced Disappearances, which was adopted by the UN General Assembly in 1992, and the Inter-American Convention on Forced Disappearances of 1994.[60] In the preambles of both instruments disappearances are listed as crimes against humanity.[61] States are obliged to prevent, to investigate and, where necessary, to penalize disappearances. They agree not to practice, permit or tolerate forced disappearances, to cooperate in the efforts to eradicate this crime, and to take effective or necessary legislative, administrative, judicial and other measures to prevent and to terminate this practice.[62]

What is lacking is the full observance of the rules listed in the Declaration and the Convention. For example, in the former Yugoslavia, between 1991 and 1995, an estimated 20 000 persons disappeared or were missing.[63] States are by no means always prepared to cooperate in looking for the disappeared. The UN-appointed expert in a special procedure for missing persons in Yugoslavia, Dr Manfred Nowak, resigned from his position in April 1997, because a number of states, including Yugoslavia and the United States, had been unwilling to help him in his work.[64]

Although disappearances have become less frequent than during the time when in most Latin American countries military regimes were in power, they have not fully disappeared. They remain a gross violation of human rights that should be fully eliminated.

CONCLUSION

Gross and systematic violations, such as the violation of the right to life, torture, genocide and disappearances, take place all over the world. International human rights standards leave no doubt about the non-acceptability of such practices. A beginning has been made with establishing instruments to fight such violations. Among these are: the UN Special Rapporteur on Extrajudicial, Arbitrary or Summary Executions, the UN Committee against Torture, the UN Special Rapporteur on Torture, the European Committee to Prevent Torture, the International Tribunals on the Former Yugoslavia and on Rwanda, and the UN Working Group on Involuntary Disappearances. Their means and possibilities are still far from sufficient. Governments should make the greatest possible effort to help implement international standards in

this field and thereby honour their treaty obligations. Those governments that have not yet ratified the said treaties should be urged to do
so immediately. Non-governmental organizations must make a sustained
effort to remind governments of their legal obligations. The victims
of gross and systematic violations and their surviving relatives are
entitled to no less.

4 Economic and Social Rights

INTRODUCTION

The previous chapter dealt with gross violations of civil and political rights. But economic and social (as well as cultural)[1] rights are human rights as well. This has been established in a great number of international declarations and treaties. *All* human rights, according to the Final Declaration of the World Conference on Human Rights in Vienna (1993), must be treated by the international community globally in a fair and equal manner, on the same footing, and with the same emphasis.[2] The word 'all' refers to the whole of civil and political, economic, social and cultural, as well as collective rights.

In his famous speech of 6 January 1941, United States President Franklin Delano Roosevelt referred to four freedoms, among which he explicitly included 'freedom from want'.[3] The Preamble of the Universal Declaration of Human Rights speaks of the promotion of social progress and better standards of life in larger freedom. These are further elaborated in the Declaration in Article 23 (the right to work), Article 24 (the right to rest and leisure), Article 26 (the right to education), and especially in the central Article 25, the first paragraph of which states:

> Everyone has the right to a standard of living adequate for the health and well-being of himself and of his family, including food, clothing, housing and medical care and necessary social services, and the right to security in the event of unemployment, sickness, disability, widowhood, old age or other lack of livelihood in circumstances beyond his control.

The Commission on Human Rights, which was established pursuant to the Charter of the United Nations (Article 68), has worked for many years at the formulation of the most important human rights in treaty form. This led in 1966 to the two well-known covenants, one on civil and political rights, and the other on economic, social and cultural rights. The Soviet Union and its allies had preferred the incorporation of all human rights in one treaty, as in their view economic and social rights were indispensable for the exercise of civil and political rights. The western states preferred two separate treaties, because, in their view, the supervision of these rights called for an entirely different approach. Civil and political rights could be guaranteed in an absolute sense, whereas the fulfilment of economic and social rights depended on the economic and social circumstances in the country concerned. Another important reason was that the United States showed great reluctance to recognize economic and social rights as human rights. To this day, it views this category as policy aims or aspirations, not as legally enforceable human rights.[4] The 142 states that have ratified the Covenant (2000), clearly see this matter in a different light.

Human rights that have come later into existence, such as the Convention on the Rights of the Child, comprise, in addition to civil and political rights, also a number of economic and social rights, including the right to health, social security, an adequate standard of living, the right to education, and protection against economic exploitation. The Convention on the Elimination of All Forms of Racial Discrimination and the one on the Elimination of All Forms of Discrimination against Women, contain specific references to the equal enjoyment of economic, social and cultural rights.

In the debates about the observance of human rights, the observance of economic and social rights is still receiving less attention than the observance of civil and political rights.[5] Perhaps this is caused by a failure to recognize phenomena such as poverty, malnutrition, illiteracy and unemployment as human rights problems.[6] This is manifestly wrong. It needs little imagination to see that the right to life, which is generally considered as one of the classical civil rights, is closely linked to the (economic) rights to food, housing and healthcare. They are inseparable.

The realization of economic, social and cultural rights demands both government abstention and government intervention. The authorities thus have both positive as well as negative obligations in this field. At the request of the Sub-Commission on Prevention of Discrimination and Protection of Minorities, the Norwegian human rights expert Asbjørn Eide in 1983 designed a typology of government obligations in the field of economic, social and cultural rights. He distinguished:

- the obligation to respect: the negative ('abstention') obligation of states to refrain from interfering with or constraining the exercise of such rights and freedoms;
- the obligation to protect: the positive obligation of states to take steps – legislative or otherwise – to prevent and forbid the violation of individual rights and freedoms by third parties;

- the obligation to fulfil: this requires states to take further positive measures to ensure the effective realization of such rights.[7]

This typology can be used in the further elaboration of states' obligations in the area of economic, social and cultural rights and in the judgement by international bodies of legislation, policy and other activities of states in this field.[8]

The Sub-Commission also publishes studies in the field of economic, social and cultural rights, such as income distribution and food. In 1998, studies have been undertaken on the right to education, the right of access to drinking water and again on the right to food.

CONTENTS

Economic and social rights deal with fundamental matters such as the right to work, the right to equitable and favourable labour conditions,[9] the right to social security,[10] the right to a decent standard of living, including adequate food,[11] clothing and housing,[12] the right to adequate health care,[13] and the right to education.[14] The collective rights to a clean natural environment[15] and the right of development[16] also belong to the category of economic and social rights.[17]

Much has been written about the question of what exactly are economic and social rights and whether they are principally different from civil and political rights.[18] The debate often deals with the interpretation of the obligations of states which are parties to the International Covenant on Economic, Social and Cultural Rights (ICESCR). These obligations are laid down in Article 2, paragraph 1 of that Covenant:

> Each State Party to the present Covenant undertakes to take steps, individually and through international assistance and cooperation, especially economic and technical, to the maximum of its available resources, with a view to achieving progressively the full realization of the rights recognized in the present Covenant by all appropriate means, including particularly the adoption of legislative measures.

The so-called general comments of the UN Committee on Economic, Social and Cultural Rights are an important source of interpretation. The Covenant on Economic, Social and Cultural Rights does not provide for the establishment of a supervisory committee, as is the case with the Covenant on Civil and Political Rights. The states parties to the Covenant must report to the Secretary-General of the United Nations on the measures which they have adopted and the progress made in achieving the observance of the rights mentioned in the Covenant. The Secretary-General transmits these reports to the Economic and Social Council (ICESCR, Article 16). In view of its considerable workload, in 1978 ECOSOC established a working group, which in 1985 was replaced by the present ESC committee; this committee began its work in 1987.[19]

In 1988, the Committee began to publish general comments with regard to the articles of the ECESCR, with the aim to assist states parties in the fulfilment of their obligations.[20] So far, the Committee has published the following general comments: reporting by states parties (1989), international technical assistance measures (1990), the nature of states parties obligations (1990), the right to adequate housing (1991), persons with disabilities (1994), the economic, social and cultural rights of older persons (1995), forced evictions (1997), the observance of economic, social and economic rights (1997), the domestic application of the Covenant (1998), the role of national institutions (1998), plan of action for primary education (1999), the right to adequate food (1999), the right to education (1999), and the right to the highest attainable health (2000).[21]

A second source of interpretation of these treaty obligations is the so-called 'Limburg Principles' which were drawn up during a conference in 1986 in Maastricht, in the Netherlands, which was attended by scholars, representatives of intergovernmental organizations, and NGOs. The Limburg Principles aim to provide an interpretation of the nature of state obligations with regard to the ICESCR and the international supervision of these obligations.[22]

Should all states meet the same criteria? Yes and no. At first sight, it would seem not very realistic to demand that poor countries such as Afghanistan or Ethiopia should meet the same standards as wealthy countries such as the Netherlands or Sweden. The Covenant says that each state should take steps 'to the maximum of its available resources', which may of course differ from case to case. This should help 'to achieve progressively the full realization of the rights'. This formulation implies a certain degree of flexibility. It is recognized that not all economic, social and cultural rights can be realized everywhere within a short period of time. There are, however, miminum core obligations which must be met by all states parties. States must indicate that they have made all efforts to meet at least these minimum core obligations.

What are these minimum core obligations? Do they differ from country to country or are there minimum core obligations that are universally valid? Some observers claim that for each country a minimum threshold should be established, for example with regard to criteria such as child mortality, the presence of certain illnesses, life expectation, income per capita, unemployment, food consumption and literacy.[23] At the regional level, for states parties to the European Social Charter (ESC), reasonable levels of implementation have been established on a state-by-state basis, taking into consideration the economic circumstances of the country concerned. The Committee of Experts of the ESC has chosen a minimum threshold per country of 68 per cent of the national average wage level.[24] At the global level, it has not yet been possible to determine such a minimum threshold. There is also the danger that these thresholds may strongly differ from each other.

States often put forward as a mitigating circumstance for not meeting, or not fully meeting, their treaty obligations, that they have been unable to guarantee economic and social rights because of reversals at the economic and social level. Against this it is argued that it is precisely in times of economic recession that these rights should be observed.[25] *Force majeure* or impotence to fulfil treaty obligations are arguments that should be carefully checked. Natural disasters or an international fall of commodity prices are relevant examples of mitigating circumstances. But a state that does not fulfil its obligation to provide free primary education, although it is able to do so, is guilty of a treaty violation. Also the non-submission of adequate reports on the observance of the ICESCR is a non-observance of a treaty obligation. It is not always easy to determine whether a state is *not willing* or *not able* to honour its treaty obligations. This calls for careful international investigation. Non-governmental organizations can assist in this process, by providing relevant reliable information.[26]

Forced eviction as practised in the Dominican Republic, Panama, Nigeria and the Philippines, where people have been forceably evicted from their homes, are examples of violations of the right to housing.[27] In a different manner, this is also what has happened in Israel, where the houses of alleged terrorists have been blown up.[28] Human rights organizations, such as Amnesty International, have launched protests against this practice, as it hurts not only the alleged terrorist but also the members of his family. They are thus being denied their right to housing.[29]

PROHIBITION OF DISCRIMINATION

Discrimination is prohibited under the International Covenant on Economic, Social and Cultural Rights (Article 2, paragraph 2 and Article

3). But also certain arrangements that formally are seen as belonging to the area of civil and political rights can have consequences for economic and social rights. This is, for instance, the case with the prohibition of discrimination stipulated in Article 26 of the International Covenant on Civil and Political Rights, with special reference to the equal treatment of men and women.[30] In 1987, the UN Human Rights Committee found that in two cases[31] the Netherlands had violated Article 26 by denying certain social security payments to married women, whereas in the case of men marriage played no role (the so-called 'breadwinner's principle'). Married women only received the social benefit if they could prove that they were breadwinners for their family – which men did not have to prove. The Committee found:

> Although Article 26 requires that legislation should prohibit discrimination, it does not of itself contain any obligation with respect to the matters that may be provided for by legislation. Thus it does not, for example, require any State to enact legislation to provide for social security. However, when such legislation is adopted in the exercise of a State's sovereign power, then such legislation must comply with article 26 of the Covenant.[32]

After this view, which was accepted by the Dutch courts and which had far-reaching financial consequences for the government, it was suggested by some that the Netherlands should annul the Covenant on Civil and Political Rights and then become a party again, having made a reservation with regard to Article 26. Non-governmental human rights organizations protested strongly against this suggestion and nothing came of the idea. It would indeed have been a curious development, if the Netherlands, which has a tradition of honouring its human rights treaty obligations, had made such an exception at the moment that the fulfilment of a crucial right such as that of non-discrimination has financial consequences.

THE RIGHT TO COMPLAIN

This is distinct from the area of civil and political rights: there exists no right to complain for states or individuals in case of an alleged violation of economic, social and cultural rights. Establishment of such a right, in the form of an optional protocol to the International Covenant on Economic, Social and Cultural Rights, would strongly increase the possibilities for UN bodies to supervise the observation of such rights. So far, states have been reluctant to agree to such a right to complain.

The Australian human rights expert, Philip Alston, at the request of the Committee on Economic, Social and Cultural Rights, prepared in 1992 a study on the subject.[33] It is partly due to this study that a cautious passage was included in the Final Declaration of the 1993 World Conference on Human Rights in Vienna: 'The World Conference encourages the Commission on Human Rights, in cooperation with the Committee on Economic, Social and Cultural Rights, to continue the examination of optional protocols to the International Covenant on Economic, Social and Cultural Rights.'[34]

The debates on the possibility of a right to complain about (the denial of) economic, social and cultural rights are fed by two draft texts: one by Philip Alston,[35] and one that was the result of a conference of experts organized by the Netherlands Institute of Human Rights (SIM) in January 1995.[36] Debates deal with the question of the justiciability of economic, social and cultural rights.[37] The view is now commonly accepted that this will depend on the nature of the case; it is, in other words a 'fluid concept'. For example, many aspects of the right to housing are in many national legal systems open to judicial review.[38] Generally speaking, the courts are reluctant to review economic, social and cultural rights, in view of the alleged vagueness of relevant standards. However, this should be seen as an important argument to arrive at a formal complaints procedure, as judicial review would offer an opportunity to derive concrete obligations from vague standards.

The Dutch section of the International Commission of Jurists, NJCM, has argued in favour of setting up a complaints procedure which should be given to a wider group than only individual complainants. Such a complaints procedure should be applied first to a limited number of economic, social and cultural rights, to be gradually expanded.[39] The Dutch Advisory Committee on Human Rights and Foreign Policy has also argued in favour of such a complaints procedure.[40]

Adoption of a complaints procedure for violations of economic, social and cultural rights is, for the time being, still a matter of considerable controversy among both academics and politicians. Governments are reluctant to commit themselves in an area in which they cannot see all the possible consequences. Against this it should be argued that if, as it has often been said, *all* human rights deserve equal treatment, adoption of a complaints procedure would be an important step in the right direction.

NON-GOVERNMENTAL ORGANIZATIONS

Apart from trade unions there are very few international non-governmental organizations that explicitly work for the promotion of economic and social human rights. The principal ones are the Center for Economic and Social Rights (COHRE) in New York, the Centre on Housing Rights and Evictions (CHRE) that deals with the right to housing,[41] and Foodfirst Information and Action Network (FIAN), which investigates fundamental causes of and solutions to hunger and poverty in the world and works for the right to food as a human right. The Organisation Internationale pour le Développement de la Liberté d'Enseignement (OIDLE) and the World University Service (WUS) are active in the field of the right to education. Although they do useful work, they are small organizations with a delicate financial basis, lacking sufficient mass support in society. The major human rights organizations pay relatively little attention to economic, social and cultural rights.[42]

Non-governmental organizations play an important role in the implementation of human rights. They remind governments continually of their treaty obligations. Moreover, they help to develop and refine international standards in the field.[43] They can submit proposals to the UN Committee on Economic, Social and Cultural Rights and take part in the general debate in that Committee. However, NGOs have so far shown little interest in the work of the Committee.[44]

The lack of large, active organizations in the field of economic and social rights, that generate reliable information, is a serious deficiency. If a complaints procedure on economic, social and cultural rights were to be adopted, this would also call for an active role by NGOs, either by introducing complaints themselves or by providing relevant information.[45]

The establishment of an Amnesty International for economic, social and cultural rights is urgently needed. Setting up such an organization need not be terribly difficult. Amnesty itself was started by a few British lawyers who were concerned about the fate of some detained Portuguese students. Their article in a British Sunday newspaper[46] led to what is now a world organization. They based themselves on relevant articles in the Universal Declaration of Human Rights. By analogy, a start could be made with an NGO on violations of ESC rights, using relevant audio-visual means, perhaps the Internet. The deficiencies in the implementation of economic, social and cultural rights in the world call for such an organization.[47]

CONCLUSIONS

Human rights concern the protection of human dignity. There can be little doubt that hunger, lack of adequate housing and the lack of sufficient health care are serious infringements of human dignity. In many cases, they coincide with a violation of the fundamental right to life. The same is to a greater or lesser degree true for the other economic and social rights. Therefore it is only right that nowadays the plea is often made for the protection of *all* human rights. This is in principle recognized by most governments. The overwhelming majority of states have recognized this principle by having ratified the International Covenant on Economic, Social and Cultural Rights. The 'Limburg Principles' and the General Comments by the UN Committee on Economic, Social and Cultural Rights have further clarified the standards contained in that Covenant.

Most governments recognize nowadays the fundamental importance of economic, social and cultural human rights. The United States government is unfortunately still one of the major exceptions to that rule. To recognize a principle is, however, not the same as to observe that principle in practice. Most fundamental economic and social rights are still being violated in many parts of the world. It is usually not easy to determine whether such violations are caused by a lack of will or a lack of capability on the part of governments to provide for the most fundamental necessities of life. The question whether failing governments rightly or wrongly refer to impotence or circumstances beyond their control should be reviewed through a careful international procedure. Governments should at least be expected to demonstrate that they are doing everything they can to meet international standards in this field.

What is lacking are adequate international supervision mechanisms of economic and social rights. The increasing importance of the UN Committee on Economic, Social and Cultural Rights is a step in the right direction. It is hampered, however, by the infrequency of its meetings[48] and the inadequate secretarial support offered by the Office of the High Commissioner for Human Rights.

The introduction of a complaints procedure in the form of an Optional Protocol to the Covenant would be an important addition and contribute to a more effective supervision of the observance of economic and social human rights. Scholars, with the help of non-governmental organizations, have done much work in drafting such a Protocol. Governments that have so far been reluctant to accept it, should be encouraged to do so.

More pressure should be exerted on governments to pay serious attention to the observance of their obligations in the field of economic and social human rights. One way of doing this is to provide reliable information about violations of such rights. The establishment of strong and well-organized NGOs such as already exist in the field of civil and political rights, would be of great importance. That might help to arrive at a really even-handed approach to dealing with the problems of all human rights.

5 Collective Rights: the Right of Self-Determination

INTRODUCTION

Human rights are in the first place for the protection of the individual. This becomes clear, for example, when reading the first sentence of the preamble of the Universal Declaration of Human Rights: '*Whereas* recognition of the inherent dignity and of the equal and inalienable rights of all members of the human family is the foundation of freedom, justice and peace in the world ... '. What follows is a list of human rights, phrased in terms of individual rights. Usually the sentence reads 'Everyone has the right to' or 'is entitled to' ('all the rights and freedoms set forth in this Declaration', Art. 2) ('life, liberty and the security of person', Art. 3) or 'no one shall' ('be held in slavery or servitude', Art. 4) or ('be subjected to torture or to cruel, inhuman or degrading treatment or punishment', Art. 5).

A major objective of human rights is to protect the individual human being against abuse of power by the authorities ('vertical rights') or by other individuals ('horizontal rights') and to protect against the abuse of state power. This remains true, even though certain rights are mainly or only exercised collectively. A well-known illustration is formed by Article 20 of the Universal Declaration of Human Rights: 'Everyone has the right to freedom of peaceful assembly and association.' For the exercise of that right, at least two persons are needed, as an individual cannot assemble or associate on his own. But the right is formulated as pertaining to individuals. This is even true for the rights of minorities, an obvious example of collectivities. Article 27 of the International Covenant on Civil and Political Rights, which deals with this matter, does not refer to 'minorities', but to 'persons belonging to [...] minorities'. In other words: at the time of drafting the Covenant, an explicit choice was made to formulate the rights of minorities in individual terms. States, not without reason, were afraid that certain minorities might otherwise claim rights from this article, which could turn out to be negative for the state (and its governing majority).

In the two human rights covenants of 1966, the only exception to the rule that rights are formulated in individual terms is common Article 1: 'All peoples have the right of self-determination.' But that formulation has caused a number of problems, both in regard to the people to whom this right refers as well as the subject that can exercise it. At the time, it was decided not to formulate the consequences of this right: internal? external? under which conditions? did it include the right to secession? No definition of the concept of 'people' was ever given. Another treaty, that should be mentioned in this context, is the African Charter on Human and Peoples' Rights. That treaty mentions a large number of rights of peoples,[1] but omits a description of the concept of 'people'. In that case too, the reason was that the states parties were afraid that all kinds of groups might present themselves as 'peoples' and make demands which the existing states would perceive as negative to their interests.

CONTENTS

Should, next to the rights of individuals and the right of self-determination, other collective rights (or group rights) be recognized? Which rights would be at stake and who could make legitimate demands to them? Another question is whether such rights should be seen as collective rights or given the status of collective *human* rights.[2] Posing such questions brings us into the realm of controversy. In the academic literature a great deal of attention is being paid to these problems.[3]

In 1993, the Dutch Advisory Committee on Human Rights and Foreign Policy was asked by then Minister Kooijmans of Foreign Affairs to answer the question 'whether collective rights qualify, in principle, for recognition, and if so, which of the rights currently styled "collective" could be regarded as true collective rights. You might also consider the potential added value of such rights with respect to those civil, political, economic, social and cultural rights which have already been recognized, and the conditions which would have to be attached to the exercise of collective rights.'[4] The advisory report, which was issued in May 1995, marks out the problem area, discusses who are the bearers of collective rights and deals with a number of concrete collective demands. Furthermore, the advisory report contains six criteria that are considered of importance for the recognition of collective rights: (1) they must have an object which determines the substance of the right; (2) they must have a subject (bearer) who can invoke the right; (3) they must be addressed to a duty-bearer against whom they can be invoked; (4) the claim must be essential to a dignified existence; (5) the claim should not be one which can be individualized and (6) the claim must reinforce the exercise of individual human rights, and in any event should not undermine existing human rights.[5]

What are collective rights? It has been argued that one should only distinguish *collective aspects* of individual human rights. This would have important consequences for the entire approach to the problem. It would mean a rejection of the idea of 'collective human rights'. In this view, there would only be place for individual human rights.[6] Within the Advisory Committee, views were divided on this point.[7] This author is a proponent of the view that collectivities should be entitled to human rights, if rights are involved that can only enjoyed by collectivities and cannot be reduced to individual rights. If collective rights could be reduced to individual rights, the notion of collective rights would have no added value. This means that the right to freedom of association and assembly, which can only be exercised collectively, as well as the right to education or the right to freedom of religion, which are usually exercised collectively, should *not* be considered as collective rights. Rights that do qualify as collective rights are: the right of self-determination, freedom from genocide, the right of peoples to development and to access to natural resources. Other collective rights are such rights as the maintenance or protection of one's culture, the prohibition of racial, religious and/or linguistic discrimination, the rights of indigenous peoples, and the rights of minorities. Van Genugten has rightly made the point that individual human rights alone are not adequate to guarantee a dignified human existence.[8]

What should be the relationship between collective rights and individual rights? Which should prevail in case of conflict? Should collective rights be permitted to harm individual rights or should the latter always prevail? To answer such questions means the making of choices. This author agrees with the Advisory Committee on Human Rights and Foreign Policy that, in case of conflict among rights, individual rights should prevail. It may even be argued that collective rights should *always* serve to reinforce the exercise of individual rights. Collective rights are then subjected to individual human rights. This preference is based on the notion that what has been achieved in the field of human rights should at least be preserved. Whether a collective demand should be accepted as a right depends on the question of whether it adds something to the guarantees offered by already existing human rights to a dignified human existence and the quality of society as a whole.[9]

Who are the bearers of collective rights? The obvious answer would be: groups, collectivities. Should the state also be considered as a

bearer of collective rights? This is an interesting question, as traditionally human rights are seen as instruments to protect the rights of individuals versus state power. Therefore the state should be rather seen as
an addressee of individual as well as collective rights, but not as a
bearer of such rights.[10]

Are peoples bearers of collective rights? Yes, if only because they are
mentioned as such in international treaties. But what are peoples?
Should an ethnic or a territorial definition, or a combination of the two,
be employed? Are Jews and Palestinians separate peoples or should
only citizens of the State of Israel be seen as a people? The answer to
this question is important, because groups of human beings appeal to this
kind of rights in support of their claims to autonomy, self-government or
political independence (see further below).

Are minorities bearers of collective rights? In principle yes, but this
approach meets so far with little support among existing states. It is by
no means accidental that in existing treaties minority rights are formulated as rights of collections of individuals. Certain states, such as
France, explicitly deny the existence of (ethnic) minorities within their
territorial borders.[11]

Should certain conditions be set as to who may act as *representative* of
a given collectivity? That would seem to be necessary, in order to prevent anyone from claiming to represent a certain collectivity. Whether
this should mean the holding of formal elections is a different matter.
The holding of elections raises the question as to who exactly is entitled
to participate in such elections. All those who consider themselves as
belonging to a certain entity? Or only those who have been admitted by
the group's leadership? Or only those who live on the territory to which
the decision-making in question refers? Or should participation be
based on old, traditional customs handed down through the ages? It is
not easy to give a satisfactory answer to such questions. It will, however,
be necessary to find such answers, if only to avoid dealing with such
matters in an arbitrary fashion.

The right to (one's own) natural resources is often mentioned as a
collective human right (e.g. Article 21 of the African Charter on
Human and Peoples' Rights). One may, however, ask oneself, why?
Why has a certain group of human beings a 'right' to the proceeds of
natural resources that happen to be present below, upon or above the
territory where those human beings are living? Why should it be justified
that others who happen to live in places that have been less endowed by
nature, do not enjoy such profits? This applies not only to oil-rich states
in the Middle East and elsewhere, but also to West European states

such as Norway and the Netherlands who profit greatly from their reserves of natural gas under their territory. There would seem to be nothing 'right' about such collective rights. An international income tax to even out such inequalities would be a much fairer solution, but is not likely to be accepted in the foreseeable future.

Collective human rights are still the subject of fierce debates that have so far remained undecided. The remainder of this chapter deals with the best-known, but also rather controversial, collective right: the right of self-determination.

SELF-DETERMINATION

From the beginning, United Nations practice has to a certain extent been dominated by what the Charter calls the 'principle' of self-determination, and what later has evolved into a 'right' of self-determination.[12] The growth in membership of the UN from 51 to 189 states was to a large extent caused by the application of the right to (external) self-determination. In practice, self-determination has been understood by the colonized peoples of Africa and Asia as the right to political independence, though the framers of the Charters had never meant it that way.[13]

In the first instance, the principle of self-determination was meant to counter the arbitrary shuffling of populations from one political entity to the next, as had been common practice throughout world history (one may think of the three Polish partitions or the French–German struggle over Alsace-Lorraine).[14] But also after the Second World War, the Netherlands government, for example, had no qualms about placing about 70 square kilometres of German territory with 10 000 German inhabitants 'provisionally' under Dutch administration, without ever having consulted the local population.[15] These practices were obviously in violation of elementary principles of self-determination.

At the same time, it has never become clear who precisely may legitimately claim the right of self-determination. The Indonesians yes, but the South Moluccans, the inhabitants of West Irian and the East Timorese evidently not; the Nigerians yes, but the Biafrans not; the Chinese yes, but the Tibetans not; the Spaniards yes, but the Basques not. One could go on in this vein, at least if self-determination is conceived as in the last instance implying the right to political independence. Self-determination has in practice been more often a 'curse than a blessing'.[16]

Appeals to the right of self-determination have often brought disasters to the people involved. The long conflict in the former Yugoslavia serves as a poignant example.

Below, the development of the concept of self-determination is considered in United Nations practice. The difference between 'external' and 'internal' self-determination is discussed, the meaning of the concept of 'peoples', the role of referenda, and the question whether the right to secession is part of the right of self-determination.

THE UN CHARTER AND THE HUMAN RIGHTS TREATIES

The principle of self-determination is mentioned in two places in the UN Charter. Article 1, paragraph 2, mentions as one of the purposes of the United Nations: 'to develop friendly relations among nations based on respect for the principle of equal rights and self-determination of peoples, and to take other appropriate measures to strengthen universal peace'. Article 55 mentions: 'the creation of conditions of stability and well-being which are necessary for peaceful and friendly relations based on respect for the principle of equal rights and self-determination of peoples'. This formulation was added by the great powers to the Dumbarton Oaks proposals, at the suggestion of the Soviet Union.[17] Self-determination was at the time not seen as a right, but as politically desirable. Self-determination was considered to embrace autonomy of peoples, but not the right of secession. The concepts of 'peoples' and 'nations' were not defined.

The International Covenant on Economic, Social and Cultural Rights (ICESCR) and the International Covenant on Civil and Political Rights (ICCPR), which were adopted by the General Assembly on 16 December 1966, include a common Article 1. Paragraph 1 says the following: 'All peoples have the right of self-determination. By virtue of that right they freely determine their political status and freely pursue their economic, social and cultural development.' The inclusion of this article at a time when many former colonies had achieved or were achieving political independence, was of major political significance. The legal content of the article is, however, in Nowak's words, 'extremely unclear and controversial'.[18]

The Final Declaration of the World Conference on Human Rights in Vienna, adopted on 25 June 1993, contains a seemingly clear passage in support of the right of self-determination: 'All peoples have the right of self-determination. By virtue of that right they freely determine their political status, and freely pursue their economic, social and cultural development.'[19] It goes on as follows:

> Taking into account the particular situation of peoples under colonial or other forms of alien domination or foreign occupation, the World Conference on Human Rights recognizes the right of peoples to take any legitimate action, in accordance with the Charter of the United Nations, to realize their inalienable right of self-determination. The World Conference on Human Rights considers the denial of the right of self-determination as a violation of human rights and underlines the importance of the effective realization of this right.[20]

That sounds like tough language, but it is mitigated in the next paragraph, when citing the Declaration on Principles of International Law concerning Friendly Relations and Cooperation among States in accordance with the Charter of the United Nations (1970), it is said that the cited passage should not be construed as authorizing or encouraging any action 'which would dismember or impair, totally or in part, the territorial integrity or political unity of sovereign and independent States conducting themselves in compliance with the principle of equal rights and self-determination of peoples and thus possessed of a Government representing the whole people belonging to the territory without distinction of any kind.' In other words, the right of secession was explicitly not recognized, which has greatly limited the right of peoples (however defined) to self-determination.

EXTERNAL SELF-DETERMINATION

In the literature a distinction is often made between external and internal self-determination.[21] External self-determination refers to the achievement of political independence, joining another state or obtaining some other kind of political status, for example association with one or more existing states; internal self-determination refers to the right of peoples to choose their own form of state and government.

In United Nations practice, the right of external self-determination has been realized by granting political independence to the former colonies of western states. On the whole, the populations of the territories in question have not been formally consulted. Usually, it was tacitly assumed that the achievement of independence for the entire territory of the former colony would meet with the approval of the population concerned. Only in a few cases were popular referendums organized by the United Nations, for example in 1955 in Togoland, in 1961 in Cameroon and in 1961 in West Samoa.

A referendum or plebiscite need not necessarily lead to independence. Higgins mentions a few cases: Cyprus, where for a long time the option of *enosis* with Greece played a role, though it ended with political independence; Gibraltar, where the population opted by referendum for a continuation of the tie with the United Kingdom; and Puerto Rico, whose population repeatedly has opted for an associated status with the United States.[22] Also the populations of the five islands of the Netherlands Antilles have opted by referendum for a continuation of its status as part of the Kingdom of the Netherlands.

An even stronger example is offered by the island of Aruba in the Caribbean, which enjoys since 1986 a *status aparte* within the Kingdom of the Netherlands. According to the arrangements that were made at the time, Aruba was slated to achieve full political independence in 1996. However, in the meantime the political leadership of Aruba – the cabinet, the governing political parties as well as the opposition – had reached the conclusion that such full independence might have negative consequences for the willingness of the international business community (especially the tourism industry) to make new investments in the island. Under the circumstances strong pressure was exerted upon the Netherlands to change the original agreement and to retain the *status aparte*. The request was granted by the Dutch government and parliament. In other words, in the case of Aruba, external self-determination has meant retaining its ties with the former colonial master.

The cited cases have not led to political independence, yet it may be said that they were expressions of external self-determination. An important indication is that the outcome has not been broadly challenged, either internally or externally. This has not always been the case. When the Netherlands, having concluded a new Statute for the Kingdom with its former colonies of Surinam and the Netherlands Antilles in the early 1950s, ceased to submit reports to the UN Secretary-General under Chapter XI of the United Nations Charter, it was at first strongly criticized by the UN and by certain Third World countries. In the meantime, however, the General Assembly adopted a resolution.[23] This resolution states that as a rule territories achieve self-government through the achievement of political independence, but it was recognized that such self-government can also be achieved through association with one or more states, if it is done on the basis of absolute equality and the freely expressed will of the population.

The General Assembly has not demanded that under all circumstances a formal plebiscite must be held.[24] Higgins has rightly expressed her doubts on the question of whether, for example, the definitive accession of West Irian with Indonesia in 1969 met with the condition of a freely expressed will of the population. The so-called 'act of free choice' by representatives of the people of West Irian was strongly manipulated by the Indonesian government. This was clearly not a case of external self-determination, but neither the chosen procedure nor its result were internationally challenged. In this regard, the case of West Irian is quite different from that of East Timor. There, also the population has not been given the opportunity of making a free choice, but in that case the decision-making process continues to be internally challenged, both because of the continued internal armed struggle and the violent reaction by the Indonesian army.

INTERNAL SELF-DETERMINATION

A useful criterion for judging the results of external self-determination may be the extent to which demands for *internal* self-determination have been met. The right of internal self-determination includes the right to a representative government and various forms of self-government or autonomy. It refers to an element of democratic decision-making, which is exercised jointly with other political human rights, as laid down in Articles 19, 21, 22, and 25 of the International Covenant on Civil and Political Rights. It ties in with the statement in the UN Declaration on Principles of International Law concerning Friendly Relations and Cooperation between States that 'a government representing the whole people belonging to the territory without distinction as to race, creed or colour' is required for self-determination.[25] The right of internal self-determination is of a permanent character and is seen as a requirement for the enjoyment of other human rights. In Manfred Nowak's words: 'Understood in this way, the right of international self-determination contains the seeds of a right of revolution against dictatorships that systematically and grossly violate human rights.'[26] The Netherlands government must have had a similar idea in mind when it placed, at the beginning of its 1979 Policy Memorandum Human Rights and Foreign Policy,[27] the following quotation from the Act of Abjuration (from Spain) of 26 July 1581:

> and that God did not create the subjects for the benefit of the Prince, to do his bidding in all things whether godly or ungodly, right or

wrong, and to serve him as slaves, but the Prince for the benefit of the subjects, without which he is no Prince.

This right of resistance to an oppressive government, which has always received a great deal of support in the Low Countries, is internationally reflected in the preamble of the Universal Declaration of Human Rights:

> *Whereas* it is essential, if man is not to be compelled to have recourse, as a last resort, to rebellion against tyranny and oppression, that human rights should be protected by the rule of law.

The right to internal self-determination is the legal translation of this principle which is a foundation-stone of human rights. The Netherlands Government in 1993 expressed itself clearly in support of such an internal right of self-determination:

> We prefer to interpret [the right of self-determination] in such a way that a right of internal self-determination is recognized in the sense that it must be possible to call a government to account. [...] Secession should only be seen as an option in the final instance. However unjust historical developments may have been, in dealing with questions of self-determination the status quo is one of the most important points of departure. On the one hand, states are obliged to take effective measures to protect the rights of minorities and indigenous peoples. On the other hand, there should be a willingness to enter into consultations and to seek for a common solution.[28]

In its advisory report on collective rights, the Dutch Advisory Committee on Human Rights and Foreign Policy has called attention, within the framework of internal self-determination, to ideas that were developed before the First World War with regard to functional autonomy.[29] This relates to the question of how all citizens of a multi-linguistic, multi-ethnic or multi-cultural society within a single state can simultaneously enjoy their cultural rights. Every individual must be free to join a particular community, to which the state consequently delegates important powers in the field of education and culture. The implication is that everyone is free, irrespective of his place of residence, to attend the school and make use of the cultural institutions of his choice. The question of whether one belongs to a numerical minority or majority consequently becomes irrelevant in terms of the scope of enjoying cultural rights. This may prevent trends in the application of the right of self-determination from occurring, while retaining the desired results.

WHAT ARE 'PEOPLES'?

Peoples are the bearers of the right of self-determination, but, as said before, agreement has never been reached about the precise meaning of that term.[30] There does seem to be agreement that external self-determination is at least due to 'peoples' (however defined) under (1) colonial, (2) hostile or (3) racist domination.[31] The Indonesian people, i.e. the population of the former Dutch East Indies, is an example of the first category; the Dutch and Belgian people, i.e. persons with a Dutch or Belgian nationality, regained their independence after the Second World War and are an example of the second category; the black population of South Africa after the ending of the apartheid regime is an example of the third category.

There are two widely used definitions of 'people': a territorial and an ethnic one. According to the territorial definition, the citizens of a country that is politically independent are indicated as the people of that country. In that sense there exist a Dutch and a Belgian people. Cultural characteristics which the members of a people have in common and which distinguish them from other peoples, such as a common past, political and social institutions, or a common religion and common symbols such as the flag or the national anthem, refer to an ethnically determined definition. Zionists before the establishment of the state of Israel, Palestinians, Kurds, Basques and Tamils consider themselves to belong to the peoples of that name. In the latter case, a subjective definition is used: persons who say of themselves that they belong to a people, are a people.

In more recent years, the international debate concerns more particularly the meaning and rights of *indigenous peoples*. Martinez Cobo has given the following description:

> Indigenous communities, peoples and nations are those which, having a historical continuity with pre-invasion and pre-colonial societies that developed on their territories, *consider themselves distinct* from other sectors of the societies now prevailing in those territories, or parts of them. They form at present non-dominant sectors of society and are determined to preserve, develop and transmit to future generations their ancestral territories, and their ethnic identity, as the basis of their continued existence as peoples, in accordance with their own cultural patterns, social institutions and legal systems[32] [italics supplied].

During the World Conference on Human Rights in 1993 in Vienna, long debates took place on the question of whether a statement should be made about the rights of indigenous peoples or indigenous people. In the end the latter term (without an s) was preferred, in order to avoid the risk that certain indigenous groups would claim rights as 'peoples'. In this connection, it is remarkable that the Draft Declaration on the Rights of Indigenous Peoples, which was adopted by the UN Working Group on Indigenous Populations in 1993, does not contain any definition of the term.[33] The Working Group uses a broad meaning of the term and has always admitted representatives of groups that consider themselves as indigenous and the work on the draft declaration as relevant for themselves.[34]

Crawford, who has edited a study about the rights of peoples, prefers to let the meaning of the term depend on the context in which it is used: 'What constitutes a people may be different for the purposes of different rights.'[35] Theoretically, this may be an attractive solution, but it has little relevance for political practice. It would contribute to clarity, if participants in the political debate would indicate whether they prefer a territorial or an ethnic definition of the term 'people'. That is not very likely to happen, however, as political leaders often have an interest in keeping the meaning of the term somewhat vague. They like to appeal to an alleged right of self-determination, leave unclear whether that is external or internal self-determination and which persons exactly belong to the people whose rights they are claiming. In that context, self-determination is more a political than a legal instrument that is somewhat arbitrarily employed.

SECESSION

Events in the former Russian republic of Chechnya have shown the tensions between the right of territorial integrity that the Russian Federation claimed for itself, and the right of self-determination claimed by the Chechnyan government. Foreign governments tended to support the Russian point of view, though considerable concern was expressed about the violent manner in which the Russian armed forces tried to subdue the rebellious republic. For instance, the Russian military operations caused the European Commission to suspend in early January 1995 negotiations about a new trade agreement. The European Commissioner for Foreign Affairs, Hans van den Broek, declared in the European Parliament: 'We do not contest that Chechnya is part of Russia, but we are concerned about the manner in which this political problem is solved by military means.'[36] The European Commissioner failed to indicate, however, how in his view the Russian government should have dealt with the matter. According to the Khasavuyrt agreement of 31 August 1996, hostilities were ended and the Russian army left Chechnya. The legal status of the territory has, however, remained unclear.[37]

The right of secession has been recognized neither in international law, nor in state practice. In the 'Declaration on the Granting of Independence to Colonial Countries and Peoples', which was adopted by the UN General Assembly in 1960,[38] any attempt aimed at the partial or total disruption of the national unity and the territorial integrity of a country is rejected as incompatible with the purposes and principles of the UN Charter. Higgins refers to the principle of *uti possidetis*, which means that existing colonial borders must not be changed after the granting of independence.[39] This principle was clearly meant to counter the danger of disintegration of young political entities as well as attempts by former colonial rulers to undermine the strength of the newly independent states by a policy of divide and rule. The examples of the failed secession of Biafra from Nigeria in 1967, and the successful one of Bangladesh from Pakistan in 1971, show that in the last instance political and military realities determine whether a particular secession is or is not internationally recognized.

Certain states make a reservation with reference to the possibility of secession. India, for example, when ratifying the International Covenant on Civil and Political Rights, explicitly laid down that 'the words "the right of self-determination" appearing [in Article 1] apply only to peoples under foreign domination and that these words do not apply to sovereign independent states or to a section of a people or nation – which is the essence of national integrity'.[40] France, Germany and the Netherlands have for various reasons formally objected to the Indian reservation.[41] India has reiterated its view at the discussion of its third periodic report by the UN Committee on Human Rights.[42]

An unusual situation seems to have occurred in Ethiopia. Article 39 of the new Ethiopian constitution states that each nation, nationality and people in Ethiopia has an unconditional right to self-determination, *including the right to secession*. If this article is literally applied, it could have enormous consequences and might lead to the division of Ethiopia into a great number of ministates. The political and economic viability of such states may be questionable. However, one may wonder what this constitutional provision will mean in reality. Article 72 of the Constitution of the Soviet Union of 1936 also gave the union republics the right of secession from the USSR. However, when the Baltic republics

Estonia, Latvia and Lithuania tried to do so in 1991, it led at first to a violent intervention by the Red Army. It was only due to political circumstances and the weakening of the central government in Moscow which led to the disintegration of the Soviet Union that the independence of all former union republics was realized.

The lack of agreement over the precise meaning of the term 'people' is connected to the lack of willingness of existing governments to recognize secessionist movements. The question of which entity is precisely the national entity which may not be disrupted can be the subject of major political controversy. Moreover, it remains the question whether the results of a consistent execution of the right of self-determination in the form of secession should be desirable. According to the Mexican sociologist Rodolfo Stavenhagen there are no less than 5000 separate ethnic or national groups in the world.[43] It is hard to say how a granting of external self-determination in the form of political independence to all of these groups would affect international relations.

CONCLUSION

The right of self-determination is part of both UN human rights covenants and of the African Charter on Human Rights and Peoples' Rights and thus belongs to international human rights. It is one of the few collective rights that are legally binding. It is often claimed by groups that consider themselves qualified for it. At the same time, it is also one of the least clear and most controversial of all human rights.

On the one hand, it is insufficiently clear who are the bearers of the right of self-determination. The term 'people' is open to manifold interpretation. The international community has so far not been able to agree on a common definition of the term. The reason for that lack of agreement is obvious: governments do not want to grant self-determination to inhabitants of their own national territories. If, on the other hand, a subjective definition were adopted, it could open the door to any group of human beings to claim to be a 'people', which would rob the right of all distinguishing features.

The object of the right of self-determination is not always clear, either. Most people tend to think that it refers to 'external' self-determination, i.e. the possibility of gaining political independence. This is always at the expense of already existing states, who will resist it. 'Internal' self-determination is less of a threat to existing states. Therefore it is easier to reach international agreement about granting such internal self-determination. It would be preferable to begin the discussion about external self-determination only after agreement has been reached about demands for internal self-determination.

Self-determination is a concept with highly emotional and controversial overtones. United Nations practice shows that granting this right – certainly within the framework of the freeing of formerly colonial territories – may have helped to solve certain problems, while at the same time creating some new ones. For some people it may be a blessing; for others a curse.

6 The United Nations Organs[1]

INTRODUCTION

Unlike the League of Nations Covenant, the UN Charter contains specific articles on human rights.[2] One of the principal purposes of the organization, according to Article 1, paragraph 3 of the Charter, is international cooperation to promote and encourage respect for human rights and fundamental freedoms for all without distinction as to race, sex, language, or religion. In this task, the General Assembly was given the power to initiate studies and make recommendations to governments (Article 13). The United Nations shall promote universal respect for, and observance of, human rights and fundamental freedoms for all without distinction as to race, sex, language or religion (Article 55). All members pledge themselves to take joint and separate action in cooperation with the Organization for the achievement of the purposes set forth in Article 55 (Article 56). One of the tasks of the Economic and Social Council (ECOSOC) is to make recommendations for the purpose of promoting respect for, and observance of, human rights and fundamental freedoms for all (Article 62, paragraph 2). This general authority was supplemented with the specific requirement that the Economic and Social Council organize a commission for the promotion of human rights (Article 68). Finally, one of the basic objectives of the Trusteeship System is to encourage respect for human rights and fundamental freedoms for all without distinction as to race, sex, language or religion (Article 76).

When the United Nations formulated fundamental human rights for all mankind, this was the first such formulation in history. The ambitious new work began in 1946, when the Commission on Human Rights was created.[3] Its presiding officer for the first few years was Eleanor Roosevelt, the widow of the United States President – a powerful personality in her own right. The Economic and Social Council instructed the new Commission to develop proposals for:

- an international bill of rights;
- international declarations or conventions relating to civil liberties, the status of women, freedom of information, and similar matters;

- the protection of minorities;
- the prevention of discrimination on grounds of race, sex, language, or religion;
- any other matter concerning human rights.

The Commission on Human Rights meets annually in the spring for five or six weeks.[4] Enlarged over the years, it includes representatives of 53 states, elected for three-year terms by the General Assembly. They are elected according to the following political-geographical distribution: Africa: 15; Asia: 12; Latin America and the Caribbean: 11; Eastern Europe: 5; Western Europe and other states: 10. It has a broad mandate touching on any matter relating to human rights. The Commission carries out studies, usually drafted by rapporteurs or by the office of the High Commissioner for Human Rights in Geneva, which is a division of the UN Secretariat.[5] It drafts international instruments relating to human rights for ratification by governments. It also undertakes special tasks assigned to it by the General Assembly or the Economic and Social Council. It investigates allegations of violations of human rights, and receives and processes communications related to such violations. Under what is called the '1503 procedure', the Commission deals in closed meetings with confidential communications about violations of human rights. Private complaints are discussed first in the Sub-Commission on the Promotion and Protection of Human Rights. If that body concludes that there seems to be 'a consistent pattern of gross and reliably attested violations of human rights', it refers the complaint to the Commission, which may then investigate further. The fact that such complaints are dealt with may already have a certain corrective effect, the more so because it is now common practice that the chairman of the Commission will announce, after the meeting, the names of the states that have been discussed under the 1503 procedure.

In its public meetings, the Commission may discuss human rights situations in all parts of the world. ECOSOC resolution 1235 (adopted in 1967) allows both members and non-members of the Commission to raise violations of human rights all over the world. This may lead to resolutions with recommendations to be submitted to ECOSOC and to the General Assembly. It may also lead to further study of the problem, for example by a working group or special rapporteur. The latter possibility has been widely used by the Commission by the appointment of *country rapporteurs* on such countries as Afghanistan, Burundi, Cambodia, Equatorial Guinea, Haiti, Iran, Iraq, the former Yugoslavia, Myanmar/ Burma, the Occupied Palestine Territories, Rwanda, Somalia, Sudan, and Congo/Zaire. Furthermore, it has appointed *thematic rapporteurs* on summary and arbitrary executions, torture, religious intolerance, mercenaries, freedom of opinion and expression, the independence of judges and lawyers, the sale of children, child prostitution and child pornography, contemporary forms of racism, racial discrimination and xenophobia, violence against women, internally displaced persons, missing persons in the former Yugoslavia, and on toxic wastes; in 1998, new Special Rapporteurs were appointed on the right to education and on the effects of foreign-debt burdens on human rights; it also approved a recommendation by the Sub-Commission to appoint a Special Rapporteur on the topic of human rights and terrorism. Working groups deal with the problem of involuntary disappearances and with arbitrary detention; in 1998, it decided to create a working group on the right to development, to be advised by an independent expert; and it agreed to establish a working group on the possible development within the United Nations system of a permanent forum for indigenous peoples. Their reports are discussed by the Commission in public meetings.

The Commission may invite representatives of non-member states or liberation movements to take part in its deliberations on a non-voting basis. Specialized agencies and certain other intergovernmental organizations also may take part in discussions on topics of concern to them. Finally, a unique feature of the Commission on Human Rights is that representatives of non-governmental organizations with consultative status are seated on the floor of the Commission. They have the right to address the Commission, take part in its debates and to have written statements circulated as United Nations documents.

No member of the United Nations, whether a party to the covenants or not, complies with *all* obligations to protect human rights. A steady stream of reports from such non-governmental organizations as Amnesty International, the International Commission of Jurists, and the United States 'watch' committees, brings to light numerous violations of fundamental human rights, especially in the civil and political realm, in many countries. The UN Commission on Human Rights also deals with a full agenda of alleged violations. In recent years, it has looked into charges against, among others, Burundi, Cambodia, Equatorial Guinea, Haiti, Iraq, the former Yugoslavia, Myanmar, Rwanda, Sudan, Congo/Zaire, and the Occupied Palestine Territories. Certain governments have failed during certain stages of the investigation, to cooperate. One of the grounds they adduced was that it intervened in their domestic affairs. Such refusals obviously hamper, but do not prevent, the gathering of evidence.

Whether parties to the covenants or not, governments usually pay lip-service to their provisions and the Universal Declaration. They also take the trouble to react to the Commission's comments, especially when they are critical. Yet such documents and recommendations do not govern all behaviour of governments, although some governments consciously try to protect at least some of the rights of their citizens. These UN documents, it can be argued, constitute an accepted normative framework of which governments are conscious and on the basis of which their subjects sometimes seek justice. At the same time, the reality of governmental behaviour tends to be covered with a great deal of symbolism, a strong feature of UN activity in the field of human rights in particular. For example, as early as 1950, the General Assembly declared 10 December of each year to be Human Rights Day, when special attention should be paid to human rights in countries throughout the world. The General Assembly named the period 1973–83 the 'Decade against Racial Discrimination', 1983–92 was the 'Second Decade against Racial Discrimination', and 1993–2003 is the third such decade. In 1995, a start was made with the 'Decade for Human Rights Education' and 1998, when the fiftieth anniversary of the Universal Declaration of Human Rights was celebrated, was again a year of human rights. Such symbolic actions – and even the very rhetoric of the Universal Declaration itself – have some meaning, for they keep alive the consciousness of the concept and focus attention of various groups and individuals on aspects of human rights violations. The symbols cannot, of course, replace actual observance by national governments of the obligations of the covenants.

The Commission deals also with the annual reports of the Sub-Commission on the Promotion and Protection of Human Rights, previously called the Sub-Commission on Prevention of Discrimination and Protection of Minorities.[6] The 26 members of the Sub-Commission are selected in their personal capacity, although it is common knowledge that some of them retain close relations with their governments. The Sub-Commission deals with studies on a broad range of human rights, which it submits to the Commission. The Sub-Commission also has an important role in the initial phase of the 1503 procedure, already mentioned.

Over the years, a considerable amount of tension has developed between the two bodies. Many members of the Commission feel that the Sub-Commission should not make pronouncements on the human rights situation in specific countries, but limit itself to its task of preparing studies for consideration by the Commission. Although, formally speaking, they may have a point, their irritation is also related to the

circumstance that members of the Commission, who represent governments, deplore the fact that certain members of the Sub-Commission,
who are often not only human rights experts but also human rights
activists, tend to take a stand in favour of victims of human rights violations. But the Sub-Commission has also been the target of criticism by
academics, who have argued that it should focus its energies on existing
implementation procedures, helping the treaty bodies with studies they
cannot do themselves and suggesting countries with urgent human
rights problems which have not previously been the subject of adequate
attention under the 1235 public procedure.[7] Only the future will tell to
what extent the Sub-Commission by reforming its activities will manage
to stay alive.

THE INTERNATIONAL COVENANTS ON HUMAN RIGHTS

In addition to its influence on many national constitutions and on UN
policies, the Universal Declaration has inspired the creation of a wide
net of new international regulations. In the form of multilateral treaties, they have been ratified by various states and give evidence of the
increasing attention that international law pays to individual persons. A
topic that has benefited from profound treatment is the discrimination
and the protection of minorities, for which the Commission on Human
Rights established its Sub-Commission in 1947. In studies and special
reports, the Sub-Commission laid the foundation for preparing a Convention on the Elimination of All Forms of Racial Discrimination that
was adopted by the General Assembly in 1965 and to which 156 states
have acceded (2000). The Convention established a committee on the
elimination of racial discrimination that meets twice a year and reports
annually to the General Assembly.[8] The Committee examines the
information placed before it by states parties to the Convention. From
time to time, it comments upon particular situations involving racial
discrimination or draws them to the attention of the General Assembly.
So far, only 25 states have recognized the competence of the Committee to deal with communications from individuals within the jurisdiction of those states and to prepare proposals and recommendations in
regard to such communications.

The most comprehensive development of the Universal Declaration
of Human Rights can be found in the two international covenants on
human rights, adopted by the General Assembly in 1966, after extended

drafting exercises by the Commission on Human Rights and consultations with governments (see Chapter 1).

Like the Universal Declaration, the covenants carry the mark of the political context of their time of birth. The then-new influence of the Afro-Asian states led to an emphasis in both documents on the right of every people to self-determination. Furthermore, the covenants state that all peoples may, for their own ends, freely dispose of their natural wealth and resources without prejudice to any obligations arising from international economic cooperation that is based on the principle of mutual benefit and international law. 'In no case', the Covenant on Economic, Social and Cultural Rights proclaims, 'may a people be deprived of its own means of subsistence.' Thus the former colonial countries insisted that nations should be able to govern their own political and economic destinies without imperialistic control.

Each of the covenants establishes a method of supervision of compliance by governments. The Covenant on Economic, Social and Cultural Rights requires that parties periodically furnish reports to the UN Secretary-General on the measures they have adopted and progress made in achieving the observance of the included rights. These reports are submitted to the Committee on Economic, Social and Cultural Rights, a committee of 18 individual experts, which was established in 1985 by the Economic and Social Council.[9] This Committee considers the national reports and submits its findings to the Economic and Social Council for consideration. ECOSOC may make recommendations of a general nature on these matters to the relevant organs of the Organization. Under the provisions of this Covenant, individuals may not complain directly to an international body about violations of these rights, though there are proposals to create such a right.[10] The Covenant serves as a standard of aspiration and a means of judging progress toward a broad list of economic, social, and cultural benefits.

The Covenant on Civil and Political Rights provides for a special permanent supervisory organ. This is the Human Rights Committee (to be distinguished from the *Commission* on Human Rights) that consists of 18 persons of high moral character and recognized competence in the field of human rights.[11] Nominated by governments, they serve in their personal capacity. The parties to the Covenant must submit reports to the Committee on any national measures to give effect to the relevant rights and on the progress made in the enjoyment of those rights. The Committee discusses these with representatives of the state in question.[12] Afterwards, the Committee issues a concluding comment, in which it expresses its views about the observance of the treaty obligations with recommendations for improvement. A specific authorization obliges the Committee to deal with complaints by a state that another has failed to fulfil its obligations. This procedure is limited to states that have recognized in advance the competence of the committee; so far, 45 states have done so.

Finally, if it adheres to an optional protocol, a state allows its subjects to communicate to the Committee that they are victims of violations by that state of any rights set out in the Covenant.[13] The Committee, after having determined that the communication is admissible under the Protocol, must bring it to the attention of the state concerned. That state must within six months submit written explanations or statements clarifying the matter and the remedy taken. The Committee then considers the communication in light of all available information and forwards its views to the state and the individual concerned. It should be mentioned that, over the years, the Committee has built up an important body of case law and it has formulated a number of general recommendations which constitute an important source of interpretation of many substantive articles of the Covenant.[14]

Capital punishment, though not forbidden in the Covenant, is limited to the most serious crimes in accordance with the law in force at the time of the commission of the crime. It shall not be imposed for crimes committed by persons below 18 years of age and shall not be carried out on pregnant women. In 1989, the General Assembly, by a vote of 59 in favour, 26 against, with 48 abstentions, adopted a second optional protocol against the death penalty. States that become parties to it are bound not to carry out executions. Only a limited exception is permitted: states may make reservations when accepting the Protocol, allowing them to use the death penalty 'in time of war pursuant to a conviction for a most serious crime of a military nature committed during wartime'. The large number of votes against (including China, the United States and most Arab countries) and abstentions shows that abolition of the death penalty is still a controversial issue. The Second Optional Protocol is adhered to by 44 states (2000).[15]

Both covenants were unanimously adopted by the General Assembly and recommended to the members for accession on 16 December 1966. Both covenants entered into force in 1976. In 2000, 147 states had ratified the Covenant on Civil and Political Rights; 99 states had ratified the first Optional Protocol. The other Covenant has been ratified by 142 states. As for the United States, President Carter submitted the covenants for advice and consent to the Senate, which ratified the Covenant on Civil and Political Rights in 1992, with a great number of reservations, interpretations and 'understandings', which set severe limits on its impact. In 1997, China has signed (and ratified in 2001) the International Covenant on Economic, Social and Cultural Rights and in 1998 it signed the Covenant on Civil and Political Rights.

OTHER HUMAN RIGHTS ACTIVITIES

In addition to the Universal Declaration and the two covenants, which cover human rights in general, over the years the General Assembly has adopted a large number of declarations and conventions with regard to specific subjects. One of the first was a declaration that the principles, including the prohibition of crimes against humanity, applied by the Nuremberg Tribunal in trying German war-criminals after the Second World War, are part of international law. This was followed by the adoption in 1948 by the General Assembly of the Convention on the Prevention and Punishment of the Crime of Genocide (the deliberate eradication of a people or their culture) that came into force in 1951.[16] In 1968, the General Assembly adopted a Convention on the Nonapplicability of Statutory Limitations to War Crimes and Crimes against Humanity, two of the laws enforced at Nuremberg; it came into force in 1970.

Discrimination on the basis of sex has also received significant attention. In 1946, the Commission on the Status of Women (CSW) was established.[17] The mandate of the Commission, which meets for only eight days every year, refers to the preparation of reports and recommendations to the Economic and Social Council regarding the equal rights of women and their equal treatment and participation in society. The Convention on the Political Rights of Women won the approval of the General Assembly in 1952. In 1967, it adopted a declaration calling for the abolition of all rules, laws, regulations, and customs that discriminate against women, and their replacement with legal protection; states are supposed to report regularly on their progress in executing the provisions of the Declaration. In addition, governments were urged in 1962 to accede to a convention regulating minimum age and consent to marriage. In 1979, the General Assembly adopted the Convention on the Elimination of All Forms of Discrimination against Women. The Convention provides for a supervisory committee whose 23 members are elected in their personal capacity by the states that are party to the Convention (2000: 166 states). This Committee, which meets annually for a period of three weeks, considers the reports submitted by the states parties on the legislative, judicial, administrative or other measures which they have adopted to give effect to the provisions of the Convention. The Committee reports annually through ECOSOC to the General Assembly and may make suggestions and general recommendations based on the examination of reports and information received from the states parties.[18] Furthermore, no less than four world conferences have been held on the improvement of the position of women; the most recent was held in 1995 in Beijing.

Another topic that has involved much activity by the General Assembly relates to the protection of rights of individual persons who are subject to arrest or detention. It supplemented long-standing treaty law by adopting a new convention on the abolition of slavery, the slave trade, and practices similar to slavery in 1956.[19] In 1959, the General Assembly adopted a declaration on the rights of the child, which was followed, some thirty years later, by a binding convention on that subject. The latter Convention has been ratified by a record number (191) of states. This Convention also provides for a supervisory committee of ten independent expert members. The Committee considers the reports which state parties must submit every five years on the measures they have adopted to give effect to the rights recognized in the Convention. The Committee reports through ECOSOC to the General Assembly.[20]

The Declaration against Torture or Cruel, Inhuman or Degrading Treatment or Punishment adopted in 1975 was also followed in 1984 by a binding convention against torture, which has been ratified by 119 states (2000). A committee of ten expert members considers the reports which state parties to the Convention submit every four years on the measures they have taken to give effect to their undertakings under the Convention. If the Committee receives reliable information which appears to it to contain well-founded indications that torture is being systematically practised in the territory of a state party, it may designate one or more of its members to make a confidential inquiry, if necessary including a visit to the territory, in agreement with the state party. The Committee will transmit its findings to the state party on a confidential basis. It may decide, after consultations with the state party concerned, to include a summary account of the result of the proceedings in its annual report. A complaints procedure by states or individuals is only possible, if the state concerned has explicitly recognized this competence of the Committee. This has been done so far by 41 states (for state complaints) and 39 states (for individual complaints). Furthermore, an optional protocol is under preparation which would allow regular visits by the Committee to places where people are being detained, along the model of the European Convention for the Prevention of Torture. This would vastly increase the capability of the Committee to supervise the observance of the treaty obligations. There is, however, considerable doubt whether many states would be prepared to accept the extended obligations under such an optional protocol.[21]

In 1979, the General Assembly adopted an eight-article code of conduct for law enforcement officials, and in 1981, a declaration on the elimination of all forms of intolerance and of discrimination based on religion or belief. In 1990, the General Assembly adopted a Convention for the Protection of Migrant Workers and their Families; this Convention has, however, been ratified by only 15 states (2000).

The General Assembly has also increasingly emphasized the importance of applying a more structural approach to the solution of the human rights problem. In addition to the struggle against violations of human rights, ways should be found to *prevent* such violations. In 1977, the Assembly adopted, for instance, a resolution on alternative approaches and ways and means for improving effective enjoyment of human rights and fundamental freedoms. The United Nations has also set up a training programme in human rights in which young academics from all over the world participate. A number of studies has been undertaken, with an emphasis on the principle of non-discrimination. Through its 'Advisory Services' programme, the UN Centre for Human Rights in Geneva organizes global and regional seminars and courses on human rights. Governments, at their request, obtain the advice of the Centre. Offending governments may invite the visit by an expert under the Advisory Services Programme, rather than having a special rapporteur deal with them.

In 1993, the General Assembly, acting on a recommendation of the second World Conference on Human Rights, decided to establish a United Nations High Commissioner for Human Rights.[22] This official has the principal responsibility for United Nations human rights activities and carries out the tasks assigned to him by the competent bodies of the United Nations. He coordinates all activities in the promotion and protection of human rights and heads the UN Centre for Human Rights, which in 1997 was joined with the secretariat of the High Commissioner to be known henceforth as Bureau of the High Commissioner for Human Rights. In 1994, the Ecuadorian diplomat José Ayalo Lasso was appointed as the first High Commissioner; in 1997, he was succeeded by the former Irish President, Mary Robinson. Ayalo Lasso received a great deal of criticism from human rights organizations for being not sufficiently outspoken in reaction to human rights violations.[23]

He was very active in paying diplomatic visits to states and excelled more in practising quiet diplomacy than in publicly denouncing human rights violations. However, he also paid a great deal of attention to the human rights situation in Rwanda, trying to improve matters there, among other things by stationing field missions there, consisting of UN observers who reported back to him. It was on his initiative that the UN Commission on Human Rights held a special session on Rwanda in 1994. His successor, Mary Robinson, showed herself less reluctant in criticizing offending governments, such as those of Rwanda and Algeria.

The United Nations has established a training programme for human rights, in which young scholars from all over the world participate. A number of studies have been undertaken under the auspices of the United Nations, emphasizing the principle of non-discrimination. Within the framework of its programme for Advisory services, the Bureau of the High Commissioner for Human Rights organizes global and regional seminars on human rights. Governments may ask the Bureau for advice. Regimes that have been found guilty of human rights violations may invite an expert within the programme for Advisory services and thus avoid the appointment of a country rapporteur by the Commission on Human Rights. Guatemala is an example of a state that has thus been able to prevent the continuation of the mandate of the Special Rapporteur.

From outside as well as inside the United Nations many proposals have been launched to improve UN supervisory procedures in the field of human rights.[24] These proposals include the following. The treaty bodies should take steps to guarantee a more thorough and punctual consideration of country reports. For that purpose they should stick more rigidly to their supervision timetables; they should see to it that the backlog of submitted country reports is more quickly dealt with; NGOs should be more actively involved in the activities of the treaty bodies; the possibilities for inquiries involving visits to the territories of the states involved should be opened; and the possibility of a 'joint' approach, whereby the various treaty bodies deal with one and the same country report at the same time, should be investigated. States now often complain, not without reason, that they are unable to meet the many different reporting obligations under the various treaties. Small states lack a sufficient number of qualified civil servants to deal with such matters. Thus the treaty bodies could help to improve the supervisory mechanisms.

SPECIALIZED AGENCIES

In addition to the instruments and activities mentioned so far, a great many recommendations and conventions bearing on human rights have been adopted by Specialized Agencies. The International Labour Organization (ILO)[25] and the UN Educational, Scientific and Cultural Organization (UNESCO) have been especially active. Some of the more important conventions are the following:

- freedom of association and protection of the right to organize (ILO, 1948);
- equal remuneration (for men and women for work of equal value) (ILO, 1951);
- abolition of forced labour (ILO, 1957);
- discrimination in respect of employment and occupation (ILO, 1958);
- discrimination in education (UNESCO, 1960);
- employment policy (ILO, 1966);
- protection of workers' representatives (ILO, 1971);
- protection of the world cultural and natural heritage (UNESCO, 1972);
- protection of the right to organize and procedures for determining conditions of employment in the public service (ILO, 1978);
- protection of the rights of indigenous and tribal populations (ILO, 1989).

A treaty for the most intolerable forms of child labour is being prepared.

These conventions also involve supervision of national behaviour by relevant international organizations and, especially in the case of the ILO, violations can lead to embarrassing publicity and even painful sanctions.

CONCLUSION

In view of the controversial, not to say revolutionary, aims of the human rights activities of the United Nations, it is not easy to make a simple assessment of what has been done. In terms of the goals set out in the UN Charter and elaborated over the years, the human rights programmes have seen both successes and failures.

The most positive result of the human rights programmes is undoubtedly the creation of international standards for the treatment of human beings all over the world. Common criteria now exist for judging whether human beings enjoy fundamental human rights. The United Nations can claim the accomplishment of making the norms more concrete so that it is possible to determine where and when they are violated. All governments accept human rights norms in principle, if not in practice. By paying at least lip-service to this idea, they also implictly accept the assumption that a limited world community exists. Moreover, non-governmental organizations rely on these very norms to take governments to task and remind them of whatever moral or legal obligations they have assumed.

A second positive outcome can be demonstrated in the remarkable increase in information that UN organs collect and distribute on the performance by states in the field of human rights. A vast reporting network includes the Commission on Human Rights, its special rapporteurs, various treaty bodies, some of the specialized agencies, the member states themselves in their national reports, various UN publications and, more recently, the activities of the High Commissioner for Human Rights. These efforts are again supplemented by extensive information-gathering on the part of non-governmental organizations.

Both the process of creating norms and the monitoring of the performance of states have encouraged the active participation of non-governmental organizations, such as Amnesty International, the International Commission of Jurists, and the various 'watch' committees. They constantly demand more effective enforcement and protection of human rights. They attempt to influence the United Nations directly through persuasion and indirectly through the member governments.

An example of successful collaboration between one such organization, Amnesty International, and the UN system, can be found in the adoption by the General Assembly in 1984 of the Convention against Torture and Other Cruel, Inhuman or Degrading Treatment or Punishment.[26] This Convention condemns acts of torture as a denial of fundamental rights and of the purposes of the UN, and urges states to take measures against such violations. Similarly, relief organizations have been active partners of UNHCR in its efforts to succour those who flee from massive denial of their rights. These private organizations, such as Catholic Relief Services or the International Rescue Committee, have helped to spread consciousness of the international norms of human rights.

Yet the performance of the United Nations in supervising and controlling the actual performance of states in the human rights field must be accounted as much less positive than the formulation of norms. Even when violations of human rights can be pinpointed as to time and place, this does not necessarily ensure that UN organs will deal with them in an objective manner. Some of the worst offenders in the field of human rights are members of the Commission on Human Rights, where their representatives make pious statements. Whether or not a case will be considered by a UN organ depends more on political factors than on the nature of the alleged violation. The apartheid policies of South Africa (in the past), or human rights violations by the Israeli forces in the Occupied Territories have unfailingly figured highly on the agenda, while at the same time dramatic violations taking place in countries such as China or Ethiopia remain unchecked by UN action. Only after Idi Amin was removed from power in Uganda were his government's murderous transgressions of human rights norms publicly taken up in UN forums. The same is true of the massive-scale killings by the regime of the late Pol Pot in Cambodia. Within the Commission on Human Rights, debates have a predominantly political character, as governments try to defend their behaviour and accuse others of wickedness. In fact, complaints about violations of human rights often become the vehicle for presenting political points of view. It is not completely without reason that some observers have accused the United Nations of applying double standards.

The United Nations can, moreover, neither effectively punish nor reward governments for their degree of compliance with human rights standards. The Security Council has the right to act only when it is convinced that a violation of human rights threatens international peace and security. It stated, however, in 1991, in resolution 688 relating to the repression of the Kurdish population in Iraq that 'the consequences [...] threaten international peace and security'. This was widely interpreted as linking human rights violations with possible action by the Security Council. Not all violations can in fact be clearly considered as endangering the peace. Furthermore, enforcement action under Chapter VII of the Charter may be too heavy an instrument to be appropriate, and in any case, the powers that command the veto in the Council have shown great reluctance to undertake sanctions. Voluntary sanctions remain an option, but these have never worked well. Finally, enforcement actions may bear more heavily on those who already suffer than on those who cause the difficulties. For example, severe economic sanctions against South Africa would have seriously affected the majority population of blacks, while whites might have been better able to protect themselves. Nevertheless, black African leaders always strongly favoured sanctions for want of more effective means for ending apartheid.

Despite the difficulty of securing a high level of compliance with human rights norms, the importance of UN activities in this field should not be underestimated. The ideas on which such work is based may take on a life of their own, just as did the French Declaration of the Rights of Man and the Citizen and the US Declaration of Independence. They matured over decades, slowly entered law and practice, and eventually became the actual limit on the behaviour of governments. The possibility of a similar development should not be excluded for the human rights norms developed within the framework of the United Nations.

7 Regional Supervisory Mechanisms

THE COUNCIL OF EUROPE[1]

Most of the member-states of the Council of Europe are also parties to the Convention for the Protection of Human Rights and Fundamental Freedoms (ECHR) of 1950.[2] It has become a precondition of membership that a new member-state will ratify the Convention as well. In 2000, 41 states were parties to the ECHR. The Convention contains a great number of provisions for the protection of civil and political rights. These include the right to life (Art. 2), freedom from torture and inhuman or degrading treatment or punishment (Art. 3), prohibition of slavery and servitude (Art. 4), liberty and security of the person (Art. 5), a fair trial within a reasonable time (Art. 6), no punishment without law (Art. 7), the right to respect for private and family life (Art. 8), freedom of thought, conscience and religion (Art. 9), freedom of expression (Art. 10), freedom of assembly and association (Art. 11), and the right to marry (Art. 12). In the First Protocol, the following rights were added: property, education, and free and secret elections. The Fourth Protocol provides for the prohibition of imprisonment for debt and the right to freedom of movement.

The supervision of the obligations of the Convention is exercised by the European Court of Human Rights.[3] All states parties to the Convention have now accepted this individual right of complaint. The major part of submitted petitions has, for various reasons, been considered inadmissible. If a complaint is considered admissible, the court tries first to reach a friendly settlement. If that turns out not to be possible, it draws up a report on the facts and gives its opinion as to whether there has been a breach by the state concerned of its obligations under the Convention.

The Convention also provides for the possibility of an inter-state complaint. Every state party to the Convention has the right to lodge with the Court a complaint of any alleged breach of the Convention by any other state party. This provision has not remained a dead letter. In 1967, Denmark, Norway, Sweden and the Netherlands submitted an inter-state complaint against Greece, because of the human rights situation under the military regime that governed the country at the time.

Greece thereupon withdrew from the Council of Europe, but the Commission on Human Rights nevertheless submitted a report in which it concluded that a number of human rights violations, including torture, had taken place. In 1982, Denmark, Norway, Sweden, France and the Netherlands submitted an inter-state complaint against Turkey claiming that human rights under the Convention were being violated by the Turkish military regime. This complaint led to a friendly settlement in 1985 whereby Turkey committed itself to report periodically on the measures it had taken with regard to its internal law and practice so as to ensure the effective implementation of the provisions of the Convention, especially with regard to conditions and procedures of detention.[4] Turkey has submitted three such reports. Since then, the inter-state complaint procedure has not been used, although one might argue that, for example in the case of Turkey, there was ample reason to do so.

The number of members of the European Court, who are elected by the Parliamentary Assembly, is equal to the number of members of the Council of Europe. In practice, each member of the Council appoints one member of the Court. Membership of the Court is now a full-time function.[5] The Court may receive applications from any person, non-governmental organization or group of individuals, claiming to be the victim of a violation by one of the state parties, provided that all domestic remedies have been exhausted. It sits in committees of three judges, in Chambers of seven judges and in a Grand Chamber of 17 judges.

There is no right of appeal against decisions of the Court. The states undertake to abide by the decision of the Court in any case to which they are parties. The Court is not authorized, however, to quash decisions of national courts or to review national legislation. Decisions of the Commission and the Court may have important consequences. An example was the judgement of 1976 on interrogation techniques used by British military and police in Northern Ireland. The Commission considered this a matter of torture, while the Court decided that it amounted to inhuman treatment. Other important decisions dealt with the prohibition of corporal punishment, the prohibition of certain measures of secret surveillance such as wire-tapping, the stopping and delaying of correspondence, freedom of the press, fair trial, and respect for family life.[6]

The supervision mechanisms of the European Convention are the most extensive and most effective existing procedures of implementation of international human rights standards. For a number of years already, the system has suffered from its own success. So many appeals are made to the European judicial organs that considerable delays have occurred in the handling of the cases.[7] In 1986, the Commission registered 706 cases, of which 469 were declared non-admissible, and 42 admissible; for 1996 these figures had grown to respectively 4758, 2776 and 624.[8] In 1986, the Court decided on 17 cases; in 1996 this figure had grown to 72, while on 1 January 1997, 145 cases were pending before the Court.[9]

The Eleventh Protocol is supposed to help to solve the problems of overburdening and to increase procedural efficiency. It has all the characteristics of a political compromise between those who wanted to maintain two separate bodies and those in favour of a merger. It is highly questionable whether the merger of the Commission and the Court, as now arranged, will offer a solution to the problems of overburdening. Not only will the Court under the new system have to decide both on the admissibility as well as on the merits of the case, but it will also have to decide on the granting of financial compensation to possible victims. Also one and the same organ may be asked to hold a second hearing on the same case.[10] Obviously, the increase in the number of states parties, especially from Eastern Europe[11] will mean an increase in the number of cases that will be submitted to the Court. Only time will tell whether the Court will be able to meet this increased workload, while maintaining the quality of its jurisdiction.

THE EUROPEAN UNION[12]

The original treaties which form the basis of the European Community (now the European Union) do not contain specific references to human rights. In the beginning, human rights did not constitute a major field of activities of the European Community.[13] In later years this has changed, however. In the course of time, the Council of Ministers, the European Commission and the European Parliament have adopted a number of joint declarations on the subject of human rights.[14]

Originally, the European Parliament and the governments meeting in the framework of European Political Cooperation (EPC) were the bodies that paid most attention to human rights. The Treaty on European Union ('Maastricht Treaty'), which entered into force in November 1993, provides for a Common Foreign and Security Policy. Its objectives include explicitly 'to develop and consolidate democracy and the rule of law, and respect for human rights and fundamental freedoms'.[15] However, at the time of writing most of this common European foreign and security policy is still very much in a preparatory stage. For the time being, foreign policy-making remains more a matter of intergovernmental cooperation than of Union policy.

During meetings of international organizations and at international conferences, EU member-states meet to exchange information and for mutual consultations. In meetings of the UN Commission on Human Rights, the country that holds the presidency of the Council of Ministers issues joint statements on behalf of the EU. Sometimes, the members of the European Union introduce common draft-resolutions.[16] In 1997, the European Commission for the first time itself took the floor in the UN Commission on Human Rights. Commissioner Hans van den Broek discussed a number of activities of the EU in the field of human rights, including its support of international and regional initiatives (international criminal tribunals and the dispatch of observers), positive measures to improve the human rights situation in developing countries, assistance in elections and measures to prevent and limit conflicts.[17]

The activities of the European Union in the field of human rights have led to what can at best be termed a 'mixed result'.[18] Though there are by now a large number of handsome statements and declarations with regard to the importance of maintaining human rights in the world, it is usually left to the member-states to draw concrete policy conclusions. The member-states are often reluctant to do so, as was recently shown in the case of China.[19] On the other hand, there are only limited possibilities for the member-states to conduct their own policies. This is especially true in the field of international trade which has to a large extent become common European policy, which, for example, makes it impossible for a member-state acting on its own to apply economic sanctions to a third state. There is, however, not yet a true Common Foreign and Security Policy, as was agreed in the Maastricht Treaty.

THE ORGANIZATION FOR SECURITY AND COOPERATION IN EUROPE[20]

The Final Act of the Helsinki Conference on Security and Cooperation in Europe (CSCE) of 1975 was originally signed by all European states except Albania, plus the United States and Canada.[21] It contains two principles which at first sight seem to contradict each other. The sixth principle deals with non-intervention in internal affairs:

> The participating States will refrain from any intervention, direct or indirect, individual or collective, in the internal or external affairs

falling within the domestic jurisdiction of another participating State, regardless of their mutual relations.

This would mean that supervision over human rights would be left to the states themselves. Human rights are mentioned in the seventh principle that deals with respect for human rights and fundamental freedoms, including the freedom of thought, conscience, religion or belief:

> The participating States will respect human rights and fundamental freedoms, including the freedom of thought, conscience, religion or belief, for all without distinction as to race, sex, language or religion.

No rank order was established among the principles. The Helsinki Final Act even explicitly excluded such a rank order:

> All the principles set forth above are of primary significance and, accordingly, they will be equally and unreservedly applied, each of them being interpreted taking into account the others.

The human rights paragraphs in the Final Act gained considerably in importance, when dissident groups in the Soviet Union and other East European countries began to use these texts to call their own governments to account over their violations of human rights. 'Helsinki monitoring groups', including 'Charter 77' in Czechoslovakia, were established, which aimed at supervising their governments in this respect. The activities of these groups were greatly hindered by the governments; many of their members were arrested. Under the regime of Leonid Brezhnev in the Soviet Union most of these groups had to stop their activities.

If intervention takes place through the use of non-violent means, this would mean that the sixth principle of the Helsinki Final Act cannot be used to prevent other countries from commenting on the lack of implementation of the human rights provisions that are mentioned in the seventh principle.

The Concluding Document of the OSCE follow-up meeting in Vienna, which was approved in January 1989, contained numerous detailed provisions on human rights. A new mechanism was developed to handle specific violations within the human dimension. This mechanism contained the following provisions:

- participating states are obliged to react to requests for information about the human dimension by other participating states;
- they must be willing to hold bilateral meetings about such issues;

- each participating state is entitled to inform all other participating states about the questions concerned;
- finally, participating states were entitled to raise such issues at the annual conferences on the human dimension and the next OSCE follow-up meeting.

These provisions were further elaborated and refined at the meetings on the human dimension, held in Paris (1989), Copenhagen (1990) and Moscow (1991) and at the follow-up meeting in Helsinki (1992). In Helsinki, it was decided to continue to hold annual implementation meetings on human dimension issues. The main task of these meetings will be to review implementation of all OSCE human dimension commitments, while indirectly a further development of these commitments is also provided for.[22] At the summit conference in Budapest in December 1994 it was decided to change the name from *Conference* into *Organization* for Security and Cooperation in Europe; this change of name was not meant to have any legal consequences, however.[23]

The OSCE was closely involved in trying to find solutions to the conflicts in the Armenian enclave of Nagorno-Karabakh in Azerbaijan and the conflict about the Russian republic of Chechnya, where serious violations of human rights were committed. The organization tried to mediate as much as possible, in both cases with varying success.[24] The same is largely true for OSCE activities in the conflict in the former Yugoslavia. The elections that were held in September 1996 under the auspices of the OSCE in Bosnia-Herzegovina, were termed 'free and fair', though doubts were expressed by expert observers.[25]

At the follow-up conference in Helsinki in 1992, a Dutch proposal was adopted to establish a High Commissioner on National Minorities. The former Dutch Minister of Foreign Affairs, Dr Max van der Stoel, was appointed as the first – and so far only – person to occupy this position. He carries out his activities beyond the glare of publicity, using the technique of 'quiet diplomacy'. Within the framework of conflict prevention he concentrates on 'early warnings' and, where necessary, 'early actions', whenever the position of any national minority in Europe leads to tensions. This means a dual task: on the one hand, he must try to contain such tensions, if they fall within his mandate; on the other hand, he must warn the OSCE if tensions increase to such a point that he is no longer able to contain them. Dr Van der Stoel's actions have received wide appreciation and he is supposed to have succeeded in containing a number of potential conflicts. The latter is difficult to prove. His successes consist of *preventing events from occurring* that, in the absence of his activities, would have taken place. The number of countries where he has been involved, is quite impressive. They include: Albania, Croatia, Estonia, Macedonia, Hungary, Kazakhstan, Kirghizia, Latvia, Lithuania, Moldova, Romania, Slovakia, and Ukraine.[26] It is striking that the activities of the High Commissioner involve exclusively countries in Central and Eastern Europe. For involvement with minorities in Western Europe or North America the political support is clearly lacking.[27]

The OSCE has so far only fulfilled a limited role in the field of human rights supervision. It functions mostly as a forum, where states, if they feel the need, can consult each other. If so asked, it makes observers available to monitor the observance of agreements in the field of human rights, including the organization of elections. The best results so far have been booked through the activities of the High Commissioner on National Minorities. This raises the question, however, of to what extent this has been due to the personal qualities of Dr Van der Stoel. His successor, the Swedish diplomat Ralf Ikeus, will not find it easy to step into his shoes.

THE ORGANIZATION OF AMERICAN STATES[28]

In 1948, the Charter of the Organization of American States (OAS) was adopted, together with the American Declaration of the Rights and Duties of Man as a set of standards in the field of human rights. In 1959, the Inter-American Commission on Human Rights was created. In 1969, the American Convention on Human Rights was adopted, creating the Inter-American Court of Human Rights, while the Commission continued to coexist. The provisions of the OAS Charter and the American Declaration of the Rights and Duties of Man, which apply to all members of the OAS, are supervised by the Inter-American Commission. The provisions of the Convention, which only apply to the states parties to the Convention, are supervised by the Inter-American Commission and the Inter-American Court.[29]

The Inter-American Commission on Human Rights has seven members elected by the General Assembly of the OAS to act in their individual capacity. Its aim is to promote the observance and defence of human rights in the continent as well as to serve as a consultative body for the OAS in this field. It may accept petitions from individuals, groups of individuals or non-governmental organizations. As in the case of the European Convention, national remedies must be exhausted before the

Commission may deal with a petition. Furthermore, the Commission can conduct an investigation of its own and prepare a report on the human rights situation in a particular country. It may request information from the parties, conduct hearings or – with the approval of the government concerned – have a special committee visit the country under investigation. Thus, in the past, the Commission has issued reports on Bolivia, Chile, Cuba, Guatemala, Haiti, Panama, Paraguay, Peru and Surinam. Its reports are usually submitted to the OAS General Assembly. The Convention provides also for the possibility of inter-state complaints, if both the complaining state and the state against which the complaint is lodged have explicitly recognized the competence of the Commission for this purpose. However, so far this procedure has never been put into practice.

The Inter-American Court consists of seven members elected by a majority vote of the states parties to the Convention. It decides on disputes brought before it by states parties to the Convention or by the Inter-American Commission relating to charges that a state party has violated the Convention. It may also render advisory opinions at the request of any member of the OAS or organs of the organization on the interpretation of the Convention and other human rights treaties, and on the conformity of national laws of the states with these treaties. For many years, the Court had ruled on very few contentious cases, but more recently its workload has increased.[30] Thus it has rendered verdicts against Honduras in relation to three cases of disappearances, two cases against Surinam, and one each against Argentina, Colombia, Ecuador, Peru and Venezuela. The governments of Argentina and Venezuela have accepted the facts of the cases brought against them. A number of other cases are still pending. Toward the end of 2000, 21 of the 25 states parties to the Convention had recognized the jurisdiction of the Court with regard to the interpretation and application of the Convention.

The Inter-American Commission is different from the European Commission in that it can itself take the initiative to deal with a case and a person need not be a victim himself to bring a case before the Commission. This gives it a stronger position in the protection of human rights. When conducting an investigation in a particular country, the Commission may accept all information that is supplied, irrespective of formal criteria of admissibility as evidence. Such local visits provide the Commission with the opportunity to become acquainted with the details of gross human rights violations. The affected governments have not taken kindly to the active role of the Inter-American human rights organs. At meetings of the OAS General Assembly, the Inter-American Commission has been severely criticized for its 'deviation from international law'.

In 1987, the Inter-American Convention to Prevent and Punish Torture entered into force; 13 states are parties to that Convention. A convention to prevent and punish forced disappearances of persons was adopted in 1994. A convention of the Prevention, Punishment and Elimination of Violence against Women has been ratified by 29 states (2000). An Inter-American Declaration for the Protection of Indigenous Peoples is under discussion.

The Inter-American organs in the field of human rights have gained prestige over the years. This is clearly linked to the fact that in most Latin American countries military dictatorships have been substituted by elected civilian governments. The strange paradox has occurred that some of these civilian governments tend to become irritated by what they see as new forms of intervention in their domestic affairs. An example was the criticism expressed by the Inter-American Commission with regard to the granting of amnesty to former violators of human rights in Uruguay – a decision that had been approved by a majority of the voters in that country. The same is true of the criticism of the Commission of lacunae in election procedures. This has caused certain Latin American governments to try to trim the powers of the Commission. Farer has made the point that it would indeed be a curious development if the very governments that had regained power partly thanks to the efforts of the Commission, were now to contribute to the limitation of its powers.[31] Another serious concern is that the United States and Canada so far have refused to join this *American* Convention on Human Rights.[32]

THE ORGANIZATION OF AFRICAN UNITY[33]

The African Charter on Human and Peoples' Rights (the 'Charter of Banjul')[34] was adopted by the Organization of African Unity (OAU) in 1981 and entered into force in 1986. The human rights listed are largely derived from earlier international human rights instruments such as the Universal Declaration and the two international covenants. Its new and 'African' character consists of the list of 'peoples' rights' in the Charter. Among these are the right of self-determination, the right of peoples to freely dispose of their wealth and natural resources, the right to economic, social and cultural development, the right to peace and security and the right to a general satisfactory environment. The term 'people' is not defined, but coincides in practice with the populations living on the territories of the states parties to the Charter.[35] Another specific character of the Charter is the mentioning of duties that apply both to state parties and to individuals.

The Charter provides for an African Commission on Human and Peoples' Rights, which started to function in 1987.[36] The Commission consists of eleven members who are elected in their personal capacity for a term of six years by the Assembly of Heads of State and Government of the OAU. It was envisaged as a body to *promote* rather than to *protect* human rights.[37] The Commission, which meets twice annually,[38] deals with communications of a state party on violations of the Charter by another state party, if efforts to reach a friendly settlement have failed and after all local remedies have been exhausted. The Commission may also deal with communications from other, non-state sources.[39] It reports to the Assembly of Heads of State and Government. Its reports are confidential, unless the Assembly decides otherwise. The proceedings of the Commission which were at first unnecessarily restrictive, were reviewed in 1995 and adapted to what is common in similar institutions outside Africa.[40]

Each state party must submit a periodic report on the legislative or other measures taken with a view to giving effect to the rights and freedoms recognized in the Charter. This obligation has gradually been put into practice, but the states have been rather sparing in providing the necessary information.[41] By the end of 2000, all African states, had acceded to the Charter. While this is undoubtedly a positive development, on the whole the system has faced considerable difficulties. The African Commission has been confronted with a chronic lack of finances. Its secretariat is understaffed and the Commission lacks even the most elementary infrastructure such as office equipment, interpretation facilities[42] and other administrative support. The UN Bureau of the High Commissioner for Human Rights and a number of non-governmental organizations as well as private foundations supply financial and organization support. While such support is of course welcome, in the end the African states will have to supply the financial means of support themselves, if only to prevent the Commission from receiving too much of a 'non-African' image.

During its twentieth session in Mauritius (21–31 October 1996), the Commission adopted a Plan of Action for the five-year period 1996–2001 (the 'Mauritius Plan of Action').[43] The Plan provides for a great number of studies and research on various topics and the organization of workshops and seminars. Priority areas are the following: comparison of the African human rights system with other human rights systems;

the setting up of thematic rapporteurs; freedom of expression, association and assembly in Africa; economic, social and cultural rights under
the African Charter; the right to development, a clean and safe environment, peace, security and self-determination; the rights of the child;
freedom of movement and the right to asylum; clawback clauses from
the African Charter (these are clauses in the Charter that subject obligations to limitations); the African Commission and national structures
for the protection of human and peoples' rights; ethnic-conflict resolution; and the prevention of mass expulsion. The Plan of Action deals
also with activities in the field of protection of human rights,
cooperation with other institutions and the problems of the Secretariat.
As a previous Plan of Action was only partly realized, it remains to be
seen what will come of this new Plan.

The Charter does not provide for an African Court of Human Rights,
but a draft treaty for such a court was adopted in 1998. So far, differently
from the European and Inter-American conventions, in the African
case final decisions are left to the heads of state and government. This
means also that the African system has, so far, been dominated more by
political than by judicial considerations. The system is, however, still
very much in development. Efforts are being made to learn from European and Inter-American experiences. Non-governmental organizations are emphasizing the need for an African human rights regime that
is truly independent of governments. The future of the system will very
much depend on the degree of success of such efforts.

CONCLUSION

The supervision mechanisms within regional organizations, discussed
in this chapter, provide national governments with ample opportunity
to develop a distinctive human rights policy of their own. They can call
attention to violations of human rights in other states, and present conclusions and recommendations. A state that is not directly represented
in a regional organ can exercise its influence in the appointment of individual experts. The point has already been made that quite a few governments may nominate persons to whom they are closely linked. Thus
governments have in fact the opportunity to influence matters.

Lodging a state complaint under the provisions of the European
Convention on Human Rights is of course directly related to a state's
foreign policy. The Netherlands Government was, for example, strongly
criticized internally when it decided in 1985, together with other

complaining states, to substitute its complaint against Turkey by a friendly settlement.

States parties to the American Convention on Human Rights may influence the activities of the Inter-American Commission by raising the human rights situation in one of the other state parties. The situation under the African Charter on Human and Peoples' Rights is not yet sufficiently clear in this respect. For Asia and the Pacific, there does not yet exist a regional intergovernmental organization, nor a regional system for the protection of human rights.

In summary, it may be concluded that intergovernmental organizations, in addition to having developed regional standards of human rights, are increasingly doing work in the implementation of these standards. Their capability remains dependent on the room they receive from the member-states to do this. That remains an important limitation of their potential.

8 Foreign Policy[1]

'The Netherlands Government regards the promotion of human rights as an essential part of its foreign policy.' That quotation is from a policy document issued by the Dutch government in 1979 at the beginning of a chapter about ends and means of human rights policy.[2] In later years, the Dutch government has often repeated this point of view in other words. It has mentioned human rights as a 'central part', 'cornerstone' or 'head pillar' of its policy.[3] These words were always preceded by the article 'a(n)'. The Netherlands government wanted to express in this way that next to human rights, there were other essential, central, etc. aspects of its foreign policy. In the 1979 policy paper, the following such elements were mentioned: national security policy, European integration and the promotion of foreign trade and development cooperation. Such policy considerations are not always mutually compatible. Foreign policy-making means a making of policy choices and a setting of priorities. In this chapter, the nature of such choices and the policy instruments that are available to a government that wants to make human rights part of its foreign policy are discussed.

NATURE OF CHOICES

The choices may be politically sensitive. Should a state let human rights prevail over security interests? Should economic interests be put at risk? Should development cooperation policy be used to promote human rights abroad? Should development assistance be suspended or even completely terminated in case of human rights violations in the receiving country? This type of question may on occasion lead to heated debates in parliament, pressing cabinet ministers to come up with systematic as well as satisfactory answers. Yet governments find it hard to come up with such systematic answers. 'One must decide such issues on a case-to-case basis', is an often heard, but hardly satisfactory answer.

Another policy choice refers to the selection of countries one should concentrate on. Should a government direct its concern for human rights to countries of whatever political colour? In other words: should it be 'non-partisan' and 'non-selective'? Should a human rights policy be 'even-handed' or is that not necessary? Should a government see it as a problem, if it is accused of 'selective indignation'? Should it be allowed to make human rights policy an instrument of security policy, which would mean that one would concentrate one's attention only on governments that are already or may become one's enemies? Or should one rather focus on countries that belong to one's own political and cultural sphere? A matter of consideration may be which policy is considered to be most effective. The Government of the Netherlands once noted 'that there is more reason to make our views known in cases which concern the observance of human rights in the Western countries with which the Netherlands has close, cultural and political ties'.[4] That is a very principled and attractive-sounding point of departure, but the question is whether such an approach can always be maintained in political practice. Criticism of the human rights performance of one's allies may be misused by one's enemies. On the whole, governments will therefore be reluctant to systematically pay more attention to the human rights performance of their friends rather than that of their foes – at least in public. There are of course always informal channels, as part of what is often called 'silent diplomacy', through which one can, beyond the public ear, express one's views.

DILEMMAS

Having to make difficult choices and setting priorities is part of *all* policy-making, but perhaps even more so in the field of human rights than in other areas. This is caused by two kinds of factors. First of all, human rights policy may conflict with the maintenance of friendly relations with foreign governments. This is especially the case, if the foreign government in question is responsible for gross human rights violations. That will call for a response by those governments that emphasize human rights as an element of their foreign policy. Their embassies will be instructed to report on the human rights situation, if necessary on the basis of some specific fact-finding, which may involve asking questions that may be perceived as unfriendly by the offending government. The latter may even see this as endangering mutual friendly relations. Obviously, these relations will be perceived as even further endangered if the questions are followed up by criticism, especially so if such criticism is publicly expressed. In the relations between the Netherlands and Indonesia, such criticism led in 1992 to the decision by Indonesia that it did not want to receive any further development assistance from the Netherlands.[5]

Another factor is that human rights policy often implies that a government deals with matters that other governments consider as belonging to their 'domestic affairs'. This means a choice between respecting traditional sovereignty and intervention. For many years, the government of the Republic of South Africa claimed that apartheid was a purely domestic matter with which on the basis of Article 2, paragraph 7 of the Charter of the United Nations, the outside world, and the United Nations in particular, had no business. Governments prefer to keep their human rights violations secret, or, if such efforts are unsuccessful, claim that it is no business of the international community. The international community, for its part, will appeal to the serious nature of the violations in question as the reason why they should be considered, disregarding the domestic jurisdiction argument. Resolutions of UN bodies and other international organizations are often cited in support of this argument. Thus it is argued, for instance, that the right to life is of such a fundamental nature that it should be considered more important than national sovereignty. That can be seen as an important argument in support of interventions by international organizations, such as the United Nations.

COORDINATION OF HUMAN RIGHTS POLICY

A well-organized system of policy coordination at the governmental level can greatly facilitate the making of policy choices. In some countries, a coordination mechanism exists *within* the Ministry of Foreign Affairs that deals with human rights matters from various points of view. The various divisions and sections within the Ministry will offer their views, often by way of commenting on a draft policy paper before a decision is taken at higher level. What is often lacking, however, is sufficient coordination among ministerial departments. This means that below the ministerial level there may be insufficient systematic discussion of human rights as related to other policy considerations. This is especially important in relation to ministries dealing with subjects such as economic affairs, international trade, development assistance and defence. At the ministerial level, the Minister of Foreign Affairs can always raise human rights concerns with his colleagues, but then it may often be too late. A well-balanced and thought-out human rights policy should be prepared and considered by *all* departments concerned. That should help to guarantee that all major points of view are taken into consideration as well as all possible means for conducting an effective human rights policy.

It is not easy to set up a well-balanced and effectively functioning interministerial coordination unit, as, apart from the Ministry of Foreign Affairs, most departments tend to pay more attention to national considerations and national interests. They maintain close relations with specific sectors of the population and interest groups, which tend to emphasize other aspects than human rights. Such interest groups often do not need to exercise undue pressure on 'their' ministry, as they already know that their views will be taken into consideration. In most countries there exist close relations between the business community and the Ministry of Economic Affairs, which tend to influence each other. It would seem obvious that in that Ministry considerations of an economic nature will prevail over human rights. What is important is that the views of these officials are confronted with those of other ministries that tend to put more emphasis on human rights considerations.

Non-governmental organizations in the field of human rights must primarily turn to the Ministry of Foreign Affairs. This Ministry, which aims at the maintenance of coherence and consistency of foreign policy, is naturally concerned with the relations with the international community. Next to human rights it must see to it that the country does not become internationally isolated. This means that it will make an effort to maintain close relations with the country's geographical neighbours and with its allies. In the case of the Western European countries, this means maintaining close relations with the EU partners and NATO allies. In the case of human rights, special attention is being paid to what are often called the 'like-minded countries', which term usually refers to countries such as Norway, Sweden, Denmark, Canada and the Netherlands, which traditionally tend to put great emphasis on human rights in their foreign policy. The Ministry of Foreign Affairs must always consider the relative importance of emphasizing human rights as compared to the maintenance of friendly relations with all foreign governments. The position of the Ministry of Foreign Affairs varies in various countries. Where it is relatively weak, it may become involved only at a very late stage in negotiations on such issues as arms exports and other strategic trade relations. That may make it even harder to give sufficient consideration to the human rights aspects of such agreements.

PEACE AND SECURITY

Human rights will not always be high on the list of priorities, even of those governments that see human rights as a central element in their foreign policy. Less will be said about human rights if the offending government happens to be a major power. Criticism of human rights of such countries as the United States, Russia, or China can lead to an undesirable increase of tension in the world. Former Dutch Foreign Minister Max van der Stoel, who is now serving as OSCE High Commissioner on National Minorities and whose commitment to human rights is beyond doubt, once wrote:

> there are [. . .] situations in which human rights policy, in my opinion, should not be given absolute priority. Would it, for example, be correct policy on the eve of an important breakthrough in arms control negotiations, to risk reaching agreement by putting forward the condition that first certain specific human rights violations should be ended? I do not think so: the interest of peace and security should prevail.[6]

Conflicts may occur between human rights and other foreign policy aims which should lead to a difficult process of weighing. Turkey is a case in point. Although for many years gross human rights violations have been taking place in Turkey, as witnessed by the reports of human rights organizations,[7] western governments have on the whole been reluctant to put more than perfunctory pressure on the Turkish government to change that situation. The state complaint under the European Convention of Human Rights by Norway, Sweden, Denmark, France and the Netherlands of 1982, which led in 1985 to a friendly settlement, has not been followed up,[8] while the practice of torture has not been put to an end. The said Western European governments have refrained from lodging another state complaint. Other western governments, such as the United States, the United Kingdom and Germany have remained silent. It seems rather obvious that in the case of 'staunch NATO ally' Turkey, security interests have prevailed over human rights considerations. Turkey has not been admitted as a candidate for membership of the European Union, but that may be due as much to the opposition by EU member Greece as to Turkey's unsatisfactory human rights record.

ECONOMIC RELATIONS

Some years ago, the results were published of an academic research project into domestic efforts to influence Dutch foreign policy.[9] This included a number of case-studies of possible conflicts between human rights and economic considerations. These referred not only to verbal policy, but also to demands for concrete steps by the government in reaction to human rights violations. It is by no means certain that the proposed actions would have been effective. They would certainly have been at odds with other aspects of government policy – in particular, the promotion of foreign trade. On the whole, the latter appears to have prevailed. The Netherlands Government was found only to a limited extent to be prepared to take the steps that were demanded of it. The case-studies show clearly that human rights did not prevail over other policy considerations.

More recently, the Netherlands Government was confronted with a conflict between human rights considerations and economic interests in its relations with China. Holding the chair of the European Council of Ministers, it took the initiative in 1997 to draft a resolution in the UN Commission on Human Rights, on behalf of the EU, criticizing China for its human rights record. Similar resolutions had been drafted by the EU in previous years – resulting in the adoption of a 'no action' decision by the Commission. In 1997, however, France, later followed by Germany, Spain and Italy, refused to support this initiative. The reason was that French President Jacques Chirac was on the verge of a visit to China, where he was going to conclude a lucrative contract for the European aircraft industry. In the end, it was left to Denmark to introduce the draft resolution. As in previous years, China succeeded in preventing the draft resolution from being discussed. It later sharply criticized the Netherlands and Denmark for their alleged unfriendly attitude and by way of sanctions it annulled a number of planned ministerial visits.

DEVELOPMENT COOPERATION

In foreign policy practice, situations may be faced in which different policy objectives may turn out not to be compatible. A choice may have to be made between alternatives, all of which have negative consequences. Such a situation presents itself when the government of an aid-receiving country is found responsible for violating human rights. Should the donor country continue its support, diminish or suspend it or terminate it altogether? An argument in favour of continuation is that development aid is meant to give support to the poor, who, in the case of discontinuation, might become victims twice: once through the violation of human rights by their own government and secondly by the suspension of aid by the donor government. Moreover, it is not at all certain that the offending government will be harmed by the suspension or termination of aid. On the other hand, continuation of aid could be seen as a (tacit) form of support to the offending regime, which would make the donor government, as it were, an accomplice in the violation of human rights. Diminishing or suspending aid can have at least a symbolic significance. The donor government thereby distances itself from the violations of human rights in the receiving country.

This type of choice presented itself in the relations between the Netherlands and its former colony Indonesia, from the coming to power of President Suharto in 1965 until the ending of the aid relationship by Indonesia in 1992. On the one hand, the Netherlands government's policy was to extend aid to Indonesia to help its economic development. On the other hand, it was confronted with human rights violations for which the Indonesian government was responsible and which were at odds with the avowed human rights policy of the Netherlands. This led to an unpleasant policy choice: what type of consequences should its human rights policy have for the development relations with Indonesia, if any?[10] A complicating factor was Dutch trade interests that might be imperilled, if the Dutch government, in the view of Indonesia, put too much emphasis on the observation of human rights standards.

In the Netherlands, relations with Indonesia have always been at the centre of attention. Political parties, non-governmental organizations, and the news media have always paid considerable attention to these relations. This is partly caused by the colonial past and the reluctance with which the Netherlands parted with its colonial possessions in Asia. At the same time, critics have not ceased to point to the much sharper way in which the Netherlands has reacted to violations of human rights in another former colony, Surinam, with which development relations were fully suspended after the killing of a number of political opponents in 1982. The Netherlands Government has been often reproached for the exercise of double standards in its relations with Indonesia and Surinam, respectively.

The suppression by the Indonesian army of a *coup d'état* of left-wing officers on 30 September 1965 led to a period of massive violations of human rights. The one-time commander of Indonesian intelligence, Admiral Sudomo, has stated that between 1965 and 1968 more than half a million persons were killed. According to other sources, the figure was more than a million.[11] Beginning in October 1965, arrests took place on a massive scale. According to official statistics, in the course of the

years, 750 000 persons were arrested. These massive numbers of political prisoners were not, or only after a long time, put to any kind of trial.
Many were detained in camps. Especially during the first years of
detention, they were badly treated. Many were tortured, often leading
to their deaths. Hygienic conditions and nutrition in the camps were
grossly deficient.[12] The survivors were only gradually released, often
after many years of detention. After their release, these 'ex-Tapols'
remained exposed to all sorts of restrictions.[13]

At the time, the question was raised in the Netherlands, whether and
to what extent development aid should be used to put pressure on the
Indonesian authorities, to get the political prisoners released. The
international position of the Netherlands was strengthened, when it
became chairman of an international donor consortium for Indonesia,
the Inter-Governmental Group for Indonesia (IGGI), established in
1967. Non-governmental human rights organizations were given the
opportunity to raise human rights concerns in the margin of IGGI
meetings, though these were never formally put on the agenda. The
human rights situation further deteriorated in the early seventies, when
death squads operated, wantonly killing opponents of the Suharto
regime. In 1975, Indonesia invaded and incorporated the former Portuguese colony of East Timor, suppressing the East Timorese independence movement. The Indonesian army also acted mercilessly against
separatist movements in Aceh and West Irian.

What should the Netherlands do under these circumstances? Economic and business relations with Indonesia had improved after 1966.
Almost 10 per cent of Dutch development aid went to Indonesia. Trade
with Indonesia rose from 450 million guilders in 1966 to more than
1500 million guilders in 1984. Cultural relations showed a growing
improvement. On the other hand, non-governmental organizations
continued to urge the Dutch government to do something about the
deteriorating human rights situation in Indonesia. Also, within the
Dutch Labour Party and the smaller Radical Party, both of which
formed part of the governing coalition, voices were heard in favour of
cutting or suspending development aid to Indonesia to express Dutch
concern about the human rights situation.

Between 1982 and 1984, a number of 'mysterious murders' took
place; President Suharto in his autobiography, published in 1989,
admitted that they had occurred under official orders. There were
reports about human rights violations by the security forces in Irian
Jaya, Aceh and East Timor. On the latter island, matters came to a
head when the Indonesian military opened fire on a funeral procession

in the East-Timorese capital of Dili, killing an estimated 100 persons.[14] Since then, both intergovernmental and non-governmental organizations have reported continued human rights violations until East Timor became separate from Indonesia in 1999.

In the Netherlands, the Minister for Development Cooperation, Jan Pronk, reacted to the execution of four former bodyguards of President Sukarno by withdrawing 27 million guilders of additional aid for Indonesia. This announcement may have been of little financial importance, but it was generally seen as a cause for renewed tension between the Netherlands and Indonesia. Pronk discussed human rights during his two visits to Indonesia in 1990. He expressed publicly his aversion from the bad human rights situation in Indonesia.

In reaction to some specific promises by Indonesia, the Netherlands Government announced in January 1992 its willingness to resume its aid programme for Indonesia. It stated that it assumed that the Indonesian–Portuguese negotiations about the future of East Timor, which were to take place under the supervision of the Secretary-General of the United Nations, were to lead to a satisfactory solution. But it added that, should these negotiations not lead to satisfactory results, it would discuss possible consequences with its European partners. This threat[15] caused Indonesia to postpone negotiations about the distribution of the new Dutch development money. In answer to the Dutch threat, Indonesia started a diplomatic offensive in order to prevent other donor countries from associating themselves with the Dutch approach. The Indonesian Minister of Foreign Affairs, Mr Ali Alatas, visited a number of foreign capitals and succeeded in receiving the support he requested. Japan alone promised $US 90 million by way of compensation for Dutch aid.[16] On 13 February 1992, President Suharto, on the occasion of accepting the credentials of the new Dutch ambassador, spoke of Dutch 'colonial' behaviour, which had become apparent from the continued Dutch interference in the domestic affairs of Indonesia. The establishment of a link between human rights and economic aid, he termed 'typically western'. The Indonesian Government announced on 25 March 1992 that henceforth it did not want to receive Dutch aid anymore and that it had asked the Netherlands to discontinue its chairmanship of IGGI. By way of explanation, Indonesia referred to the 'reckless use of development aid as an instrument of intimidation or as a tool of threatening Indonesia'.[17]

Since then, official development cooperation with Indonesia has remained suspended, though a beginning has been made with certain kinds of cooperation, for example in the field of education and trade promotion. Quite a few Dutch cabinet ministers (with the exception of Mr Pronk!) have since visited Indonesia. The official state visit by Queen Beatrix in August 1995 has given a stimulus to such contacts. Until the moment of President Suharto's resignation (May 1998), official reaction to continuing human rights violations in Indonesia remained silent.

The dilemma faced by the Netherlands was the result of its traditional emphasis on human rights in its foreign policy, on the one hand, and its desire to maintain friendly relations with Indonesia – including the maintenance of a policy of development cooperation. The problems that arose were undoubtedly made more acute by the circumstance that it involved a relationship between a former colonial power and its former possession. As pointed out earlier, the Netherlands had had great difficulty in ending its colonial rule over Indonesia.

Problems of tension between considerations of human rights and of development cooperation may also appear in relations between countries that have no such former colonial ties. In a recently published study a comparison has been made between the rupture of development aid relations between Indonesia and the Netherlands and a similar case between Kenya and Norway, because Norway had expressed itself too critically over the human rights situation in Kenya.[18] In the former case, the colonial past served to aggravate the conflict, as the Indonesians could rightly point to Dutch behaviour in the past, which had been far from spotless, if seen from a perspective of respect for human rights.

From the beginning, it has been alleged by critics of the Dutch government that the suspension of aid to Surinam, while this was initially not done in the case of Indonesia, was a policy of double standards. The Netherlands government has, however, steadfastly denied that such was the case. It has emphasized the unique, treaty-bound character of the development relationship with Surinam. Aid to Surinam was not only very extensive, but also formed the lion's share of total international aid to that country. A further important consideration for suspending aid was the seriousness of the human rights violations in a country with a tradition of absence of violence in politics. The December assassinations destroyed in one blow the core of the political opposition in Surinam.

Next to these factors, mentioned by the Dutch government, there were undoubtedly other political considerations as well. Surinam is a relatively small, powerless country, while the Netherlands was and still is one of the few foreign states that has shown some real interest in its fate. The case of Indonesia is entirely different. That country is large and potentially powerful, located in a geographically important strategic position. For Dutch business interests Indonesia is far more important than Surinam.[19] Annual Dutch aid to Indonesia was small in comparison to the size of its population and represented only a small proportion of total international aid given to Indonesia.

The debate may never end about the question of whether or not the Netherlands government has applied double standards with reference to Surinam and Indonesia. The government claimed at the time that the assassinations in Surinam had changed so drastically the situation that continuation of the aid effort was impossible. It also pointed out that, according to its policy principles adopted earlier, development aid should never be used to support repressive regimes nor lead to complicity in gross violations of human rights. The government never said, however, that it had suspended the treaty with Surinam *in order to* improve the human rights situation in that country. However, in Surinam, the suspension of aid was definitely seen as a sanction in reaction to the violation of human rights. It did at least not contribute to the credibility of Dutch human rights policy, the more so as in both cases the same kind of violations of human rights (summary and arbitrary executions, disappearances, torture, arbitrary arrests) were at stake.

The Netherlands Government had at times to face strong domestic political pressure. Human rights organizations have a relatively strong position in the Netherlands. They have repeatedly pointed to the deficiencies in the human rights situation in Indonesia. On the other hand, there were clear economic interests of the Netherlands which demanded extension of trade relations with Indonesia and an improved climate for investments. These interests were not served by very explicit criticism of Indonesian government policies, in the realm of human rights or elsewhere.

The case study of Dutch–Indonesian relations serves to show how a government that makes support for human rights one of the main tenets of its foreign policy may be confronted with difficult choices of policy. Whatever it does, it will always fall short in the eyes of some critics: either because of stressing human rights too much at the expense of other central elements of foreign policy, or because of not paying enough attention to human rights.

POLICY INSTRUMENTS

Governments command a great number of instruments which can be used to influence other governments' policy. Such instruments vary roughly from 'making a friendly request' to military intervention. Between these two extremes lie many possibilities. The late Evan Luard, a British diplomat and scholar, has presented a list of such possibilities, which is discussed below.[20]

A traditional and very common possibility is to approach another government through confidential, diplomatic channels. 'Quiet diplomacy' is the classical way in which governments, through the ages, have dealt with each other. It is a matter of judgement, which may differ from case to case, whether it is more effective to take up human rights matters in public or in private. Sometimes, a government can more easily be persuaded to make certain concessions, if there is no threat of loss of face involved. On other occasions, publicity, or the *threat* of such publicity, may force a government into action. Governments often allege that they are busy taking action through diplomatic channels, when faced with critical questions by members of parliament or journalists. For obvious reasons, such statements cannot be verified. It is a matter of faith whether one is prepared to believe them. If a minister has shown on other occasions that he is personally seriously concerned with human rights questions, he is more likely to be believed when referring to confidential approaches than if he is not known for his commitment to human rights. Even non-governmental organizations such as Amnesty International do not always act in public, but may prefer using 'quiet diplomacy'. The determining factor is what method is expected to be most effective.

A common way is to look for support among other governments. A joint *démarche* is usually more likely to be effective than a solitary action. Such countries as Norway, Sweden, Denmark, the Netherlands and Canada have often found each other to be 'like-minded' in matters of human rights. For the Scandinavian countries, this was, for instance, the case in joint efforts to combat apartheid in South Africa. The Netherlands, on the other hand, has on occasion looked for support among its European Union partners, which have decided in principle to develop a common foreign and security policy. An added advantage of joint action is that a lesser burden is placed on overall bilateral relations with governments that are responsible for human rights violations. Thus, this type of 'burden-sharing' may be rather effective. On the other hand, the wish to act jointly may take time, as it may be difficult to reach agreement.

Public statements, in parliament or at meetings of international organizations such as the United Nations, are often also meant for domestic consumption. Public statements can be used to lay down a policy line to which one can refer later. At the same time, they diminish the flexibility of a government's policy.

The cancellation or postponement of ministerial visits can be a manner in which to express criticism of the human rights situation in another country. The ministerial visit itself can also be used for this purpose, although this requires considerable caution, in view of the sensitivity of such issues. The host government will usually not appreciate clearly expressed criticisms of its policies on the part of a visiting foreign dignitary. Firm pronouncements may be applauded at home, but may not at all have the desired effect abroad. Such a visit, if extended to a country that is known for its poor record in human rights, must be very carefully prepared, to prevent it from being misused by the host country as a sign of approval for its policies. Violations of human rights can lead to a restriction or breaking-off of contacts in the fields of culture or sports.

The measures which have been discussed so far all belong to the realm of what may be called the friendly or 'soft' sector. Far more controversial are instruments in the category of sanctions. Governments are more reluctant to apply them, among other reasons because they may hurt themselves. An illustration is provided by the arms embargo against South Africa. Most western states were only willing to enter into such an embargo after the Security Council had taken an explicit position in support of such sanctions. Governments tend to hide behind the argument 'if we don't do it, some other country may'. Moreover, the effect of such a measure is often put into question. It might hurt the wrong persons, promote a 'lager-mentality' or be counterproductive. A similar argument was often heard against the establishment of an oil-embargo against South Africa.

It is rather difficult to distinguish in such debates the arguments that are based on finding the most effective ways to promote human rights from those which are used for other political or economic reasons. The discussion about the effect of economic sanctions is an old one. Would an oil-embargo against South Africa in and of itself have ended apartheid? Probably not immediately, but it might have hastened the demise of the system and have brought the regime into difficulties. In the event, international disapproval undoubtedly contributed to the eventual dissolution of apartheid, but its final termination depended in the end on the people of South Africa themselves.

The instrument of a denial or cancellation of development aid has already been discussed in this chapter. In addition to the danger of manipulation, there is the danger that such measures may hurt the wrong people – the very poor, for whom development aid was set up in the first place. Members of government, even of very poor countries, rarely suffer directly from the withholding of development aid.

It is very difficult to determine, whether in the case of gross and systematic human rights violations, the cancellation or suspension of development aid is or is not an effective instrument to restore human rights. The Netherlands suspended its large aid programme to its former colony Surinam in 1982, after the summary execution by the military regime of 15 known opponents. Difficult as it is to determine afterwards whether the instruments employed have been effective, it is even harder to do so beforehand. A variation is to decrease development assistance to a human-rights-violating country, rather than completely suspending it. Such a decrease may serve as a signal of disapproval to the government in question.

Breaking off diplomatic relations is another instrument by which a government can express its disapproval of another government's policy, for example in the realm of human rights. But this instrument can be a double-edged sword. Luard has pointed to the negative aspects of breaking off diplomatic relations. He gives the example of Cambodia, where between 1975 and 1978 horrid killings took place. As no western government maintained diplomatic relations with the country at the time, there was no possibility to even try to influence the Cambodian government. Moreover, little was known outside Cambodia of what happened in the country. Luard is strongly opposed to the breaking off of diplomatic relations with this type of regime:

> There is a double disadvantage in such situations. On the one hand, there is little external influence on the government concerned. On the other hand, the oppressed population feels deserted and without recourse. Potential centres of resistance lose hope. Churches and religious groups, without support from elsewhere, lose influence. A policy of isolating a country where such events are taking place is thus the opposite of what in fact is required.[21]

One might add that in many Latin American countries foreign embassies have often functioned as a refuge for political opponents of local repressive regimes. In communist East Europe, western embassies gave moral and material support to dissident movements. These are additional reasons to maintain diplomatic representations in such countries. If one accepts these arguments, one must give up the clear sign of disapproval which is expressed by breaking off diplomatic relations. It means, however, that the diplomatic representatives must be clearly instructed as to which activities *vis-à-vis* the oppressive government they should, and which they should not take part in.

The strongest and most drastic instrument governments dispose of to put pressure on other governments is intervention; if need be, military intervention. Intervention is some manner of forceful interference by a state in the domestic or foreign affairs of another state, in order to bring about a certain manner of behaviour by that other state. Such use of force is not permitted under the rules of international law. This has, for example, been clearly formulated in the Declaration on Principles of International Law concerning Friendly Relations and Cooperation among States in accordance with the Charter of the United Nations, which was adopted by the General Assembly of the United Nations in 1970:

> Every State has the duty to refrain in its international relations from the threat or use of force against the territorial integrity or political independence of any State, or in any manner inconsistent with the purposes of the United Nations.[22]

The prohibition of the use of force also extends to what is known as 'humanitarian intervention', which refers to the unilateral threat or use of armed force by one state against another to protect the life and liberty of nationals of the latter from acts or omissions by their own government.[23] There has been a continuing debate on the question of whether gross and systematic violations of human rights in a country entitle foreign governments to resort to military intervention to put an end to such violations. The widespread occurrence of violations of human rights in countries such as Iraq, the former Yugoslavia, Somalia and Liberia has given new impetus to this debate. Some argue that military intervention is only permitted if sanctioned by the UN Security Council. Yet, interpretations differ widely as to under what circumstances the Council is authorized to take that decision. Under the present Charter provisions, the Council can only act in the case of a threat to international peace and security.

Gross human rights violations, while threatening the life and liberty of the local population, do not necessarily pose a threat to international peace and security. Should the international community nevertheless be entitled to intervene militarily? This would clearly run counter to the concept of national sovereignty, which lies at the basis of traditional international relations and which is enshrined in Article 2(7) of the Charter of the United Nations ('Nothing contained in the present Charter shall authorize the United Nations to intervene in matters which are essentially within the domestic jurisdiction of any state ...'). An additional difficulty is how to define precisely under what circumstances such military intervention would be allowed and how to prevent states from abusing it for their own political ends. Even limited actions, such as the creation of 'safe havens' for the Kurdish population in the north of Iraq by joint United States–British–Italian–Dutch action in 1991, which was explicitly rejected by the government of Iraq, are based on questionable legal grounds.[24] In its resolutions on the oppression of the Kurds in Iraq[25] and on Somalia[26] the Security Council established a direct link between gross violations of fundamental human rights and the existence of a threat to international peace and security. In the resolution on the Kurds, the Security Council condemned the repression of the civilian population in many parts of Iraq, including most recently in Kurdish-populated areas, *'the consequences of which threaten international peace and security in the region'* [italics added]. It 'insisted' that Iraq should allow immediate access by international humanitarian organizations to all those in need of assistance in all parts of Iraq. But so far it has never explicitly sanctioned military intervention to combat human rights violations. Next to the legal complexity of the issue, there is the practical problem that it may be relatively easy to decide when to intervene, but far more difficult to determine when the task has been accomplished and the troops can leave.

History is full of examples of unilateral military intervention, often with the announced intention to 'restore law and order'. In the previous century, the United States intervened many times in Central America and the Caribbean, most recently in Grenada (1983) and in Panama (1989); the Soviet Union in Hungary (1956), in Czechoslovakia (1968) and in Afghanistan (1979). In some instances such as in Hungary, intervention took place at the 'invitation' of a local government that was in trouble; in such cases the prohibition of intervention under international law was by-passed. None of these interventions took place for the real or ostensible reason of defending human rights.

Even more pertinent to the present context are the military interventions by Asian and African states, which at first sight appear to have occurred in reaction to human rights violations. The first of these was the military intervention by India in East Pakistan in 1971, which ended the slaughter of Bengali citizens by the Pakistan army and resulted in the proclamation of the independent state of Bangladesh. The second was the invasion by Tanzania in Uganda in 1979, terminating the murderous rule of dictator Idi Amin. Finally, there was the occupation of Cambodia by Vietnam in 1979, which overthrew the even more murderous rule of the Khmer Rouge of Pol Pot. None of the intervening states based their actions on humanitarian or human rights considerations. India justified its attack by alleging that it had first been attacked by Pakistan; Tanzania claimed that its troops had invaded Uganda to punish Amin for an earlier raid into Tanzania – its invasion allegedly coincided with a domestic revolt in Uganda against Amin; Vietnam denied at first that its troops had invaded Cambodia and claimed that Pol Pot had been deposed by the Cambodians themselves.[27] The reason for these denials is obvious: to recognize the legitimacy of humanitarian intervention would create a precedent which at some other point in time could be used against the intervening state. Thus Pakistan might use it to legitimize attacking India for its treatment of its Muslim subjects or China might invade Vietnam for its treatment of its Chinese minority population.

In the way they justified their actions, the three states – India, Tanzania and Vietnam – conformed to existing practice. In the course of history the principle of non-intervention has been accepted as serving the interests of all states, because it removes a source of possible conflicts and contributes thereby to the maintenance of international order and stability – in the sense of maintaining the *status quo*.

In cases of gross violations of human rights, such as apartheid in South Africa, a much stronger line of reasoning is that states are legally bound to higher obligations than refraining from interference in each other's domestic affairs. The late British professor of international relations John Vincent has expressed this reasoning in the following terms:

> when a state by its behaviour so outrages the conscience of mankind, no doctrine can be deployed to defend it against intervention. Thus it might be argued that states had not only a right but a duty to overrule the principle of non-intervention in order to defend the Jews against Nazi persecution and a parallel is drawn and similar argument urged in support of intervention against the institution of *apartheid* in present-day South Africa.[28]

The logic of his argument leads to the conclusion that states that violate internationally accepted legally binding standards, cannot appeal to the principle of non-intervention.[29] Apartheid was a flagrant violation of fundamental human rights, as codified in the Universal Declaration of Human Rights, the two UN covenants of 1966 and a large number of international treaties. Such a flagrant violation of fundamental human rights justifies external intervention even if it belongs, as the South African Government used to claim – basically to 'domestic affairs'.

CONCLUSION

The instruments that are available for the promotion of human rights do not differ fundamentally from those serving other aspects of foreign policy. An important criterion in the selection of policy instruments is their expected effectiveness. Obviously, small states are less capable of carrying out an effective human rights policy than great powers. The then American under-secretary of State, Elliott Abrams, once made the point that the United States as a superpower considered the human rights situation in such countries as South Korea or Haiti differently from the European states: 'European human rights policy is based on talk. I could imagine, if I were Dutch, Swedish or Danish, that this would be my policy too.'[30] He implied that the United States, as a superpower, had to be more cautious than smaller states in expressing itself on the human rights situation elsewhere, as its consequences were more far-reaching. At the same time, one should be aware of the much greater weight a negative pronouncement by the American Government carries on the situation in other countries.

Small and medium-sized states may find find it useful to tune their policy to that of the 'like-minded'. The voice of two, three or 15 (the EU) states will be more influential than the voice of one. However, this may raise the difficulty of reaching agreement among sovereign units and the chance that the original point of view may become diluted. In addition, the decision-making process, consisting of numerous rounds of negotiations, is almost unverifiable. This may again negatively affect the credibility of its policies. Difficult choices have to be made between effectiveness, credibility and the necessity of looking for compromises.

Finally, there is the matter of credibility to its own domestic public. Foreign policy is not made *in vacuo*. Foreign policy-makers must take account of domestic public opinion. That public opinion is expressed in parliament, in the press, through political parties and by non-governmental organizations. Violations of human rights in other parts of the world are reported in the media and may elicit indignant reactions. This is another aspect which governments have to consider in their choice of policy instruments.

9 How to Deal with Past Violations

INTRODUCTION

What should happen to persons who are guilty of gross violations of human rights and international humanitarian law? They have committed international crimes such as genocide, torture, cruel, inhuman and degrading treatment or punishment, disappearances, wanton killings, abductions, death in detention, rape, 'ethnic cleansing', robbery and ill-treatment of civilians – practices with which we in this day and age have become well familiar. The question of accountability for such acts arises whenever a change of regime has occurred, either because of internal political developments or by means of international intervention: Argentina, Chile, Guatemala, Germany after reunification, Czechoslovakia after the fall of the Communist regime, the former Yugoslavia, South Africa after the end of apartheid – to name just a few. In some cases such persons are tried by domestic courts, in other cases international criminal tribunals are established as with the former Yugoslavia and Rwanda. In other cases a process of 'lustration' is established: a system of inspection to determine whether such persons are qualified to hold official positions under the new administration. In more than 20 countries, so-called 'truth and reconciliation commissions' have been established.

In some of these cases, actual punishment of the culprits is at issue, while in others it is mainly the gathering of information about what has happened. In many cases, such as that of the so-called 'disappearances' in countries such as Argentina and Chile, the relatives and friends of the victims more or less know already or have at least strong suspicions about what has happened. The famous 'Mothers of the Plaza de Mayo' in Buenos Aires, who held their weekly silent demonstrations,[1] harboured little hope that they would ever see their loved ones again. But what they and others who ask for truth-finding want, is official confirmation of what has happened: on the part of the government, the courts, other public officials or, for that matter, a truth and reconciliation commission. Such official confirmation may take the form of financial reparations, though full financial compensation for what has happened is in itself impossible. How should a mother who lost her son, a wife who lost her husband, be financially compensated? The most

102

extensive financial reparations have been paid by the German government to the victims of the Nazi regime: *Wiedergutmachung*.[2] All in all, almost DM 100 billion have been paid out to the victims and their surviving relatives. Not all former victims were willing to accept such reparations, but what is important is that the German government in this way acknowledged its involvement for what had happened in the period 1933–45. This in itself was more important than the actual size of the financial reparations.

A special form of recognition of guilt which has received much attention in recent years, is the offering of 'apologies' for what has happened in the past. This can happen in the form of an official statement by the newly created government. Thus President Aylwin of Chile has, on behalf of the state, offered his apologies to the victims of the misdeeds of the Pinochet regime and their relatives. The US Methodist Church offered its apologies for the slaughter of more than 200 Indians in 1864 by an army unit that was commanded by a Methodist lay preacher. The Argentine Roman Catholic Church, at the request of the Pope, had asked for forgiveness for the involvement of priests in the 'dirty war' during the military dictatorship that lasted from 1976 to 1983. The French Roman Catholic Church has recently apologized to the Jews for its silence and its acquiescence in the face of French collaboration with the Holocaust.[3] There is, however, always the problem of the extent of responsibility of today's governments for misdeeds committed by their predecessors. Is the present United States government responsible for the extermination of the Indian tribes and should it apologize to their descendants? Should the Clinton administration apologize to the people of Vietnam? Should the government of President Mandela apologize to the victims of apartheid (Mandela being one of these victims himself)? When Queen Beatrix visited Indonesia in 1995, this matter came up in public discussions in the Netherlands. The Dutch government was not in favour of letting her offer apologies to the people of Indonesia as had been suggested. Apologies for what? For three hundred years of colonial domination? The bloody subjection of Aceh by Dutch troops at the beginning of this century? The two military actions of 1947 and 1948? It is certain that some form of symbolic action may be more effective than the offering of formal apologies. When German Chancellor Willy Brandt kneeled down in front of the monument for Jewish victims in Warsaw in 1970, it made a major impression on many people all over the world.

A major problem when dealing with these matters is that the guilty ones are often persons who are also needed for the rebuilding of society.

They command knowledge and expertise which it is hard to do without. Sometimes, they are politically important persons (Pinochet in Chile, De Klerk in South Africa, the late Tudjman in Croatia, Milosevic in Yugoslavia), who still hold important political positions and will not let themselves easily be taken to be judged. Or they may hold information which they can use by way of blackmail against the new leaders. Moreover there are such considerations as 'we have to move on', 'let bygones be bygones', 'forgive and forget', 'clear the decks'. This explains efforts in the movement from 'truth' towards 'reconciliation'. The German sociologist Theodor Adorno speaks in this connection of 'false reconciliation': 'The attitude that it would be proper for everything to be forgiven and forgotten by those who were wronged is expressed by the party that committed the injustice.'[4]

A precondition for any form of investigation of what has taken place in the past is that the regime that was responsible for such acts, has been replaced. After all, it is not very likely that the guilty ones, as long as they are still in power, will be prepared to cooperate in such investigations. After the change of regime, a period of transition takes place during which society must decide how to deal with the past. This chapter deals with four of these possibilities: revenge; denial; international adjudication; truth and reconciliation commissions. The latter are discussed somewhat more at length.

REVENGE

A simple way of dealing with the past is revenge. During the German occupation of the Netherlands, the idea of a *Bijltjesdag* (day of reckoning) was often discussed. Such a process of unsystematic overall revenge was fortunately avoided, but there was something called 'Special Criminal Procedures' (Bijzondere Rechtspleging), which is nowadays looked upon with somewhat mixed feelings. The heads of *Moffenmeiden*, women who had had sexual relations with German military men, were shaved and they were publicly exhibited. It took until the end of the eighties before children of Dutch national-socialists dared to publish about their personal post-war experiences. Reading such memoirs leaves one with a sense of embarrassment about the way in which innocent children of guilty parents were treated after the war.

Revenge – however understandable against the background of the crimes that were committed – does not fit with the rule of law. If people take the law in their own hands, justice is not served, but only personal revenge or ostracism. Under the rule of law, there is supposed to be an independent court whose members, while not being personally involved with the case, sift the evidence and apply general rules of evidence to individual cases. Under fair trial procedures, the accused has the right to a defence of his choice, who is given sufficient time and opportunity to examine the evidence. Where the form of a trial is chosen for no more than revenge, justice is not served. The secret trial of the Romanian dictator Ceausescu and his wife, at the end of 1989, which led to their execution, has become notorious. That 'trial' was in fact pure revenge. Human rights organizations, such as Amnesty International, who held no sympathy whatever towards the accused, have rightly protested against its unfairness. More recently, trials of Bosnian Muslims in Serb-held Bosnia have similarly been criticized for their lack of fairness.

DENIAL

In contrast to those who wish to take revenge, there are those who deny that in the past anything wrong has taken place, or that, if such was the case, the people of the present have anything to do with it. The most extreme are those who deny the existence of Nazi extermination camps (Holocaust-denial). Until quite recently, such thinking could be dismissed as held only by a few neo-Nazi freaks, but one can no longer close one's eyes to such ideas, since a highly respected person such as French Abbé Pierre expressed sympathy for them. In Germany, the expression of such ideas is a criminal offence,[5] which raises of course important problems such as the limits of freedom of expression. I shall mention two cases of such denial.

In Japan after the Second World War, war crimes trials were held, as in Nuremberg, by an international tribunal, entirely composed of non-Japanese, dealing with the trial of individual war criminals. Unlike post-war Germany, in Japan no official recognition of any form of 'war guilt' has been expressed. On the contrary, to the great irritation of other Asian countries, such as China and Korea, which had suffered greatly from Japanese atrocities during the war, Japanese leaders tended to deny any form of guilt or complicity with violations of humanitarian law during the Second World War. Repeatedly, protests were lodged against the presentation of the war in Japanese schoolbooks, which apparently showed little understanding for Japanese guilt.[6] This has come up repeatedly in the case of the so-called 'comfort women', about 200 000 mainly Asian women who during the Japanese occupation were forced into prostitution with Japanese military men. The Japanese government has recently apologized for this behaviour and helped to set up a private fund to compensate the women. Most of the survivors have refused the money, saying they wanted direct compensation from the Japanese government itself. In January 1997, Japan's chief government spokesman was quoted by Japanese news media as saying that the Asian women sent to front-line brothels were simply trying to make money and were no different from Japanese prostitutes who were operating legally in Japan at the time. Prime Minister Hashimoto later publicly apologized to the South Korean President for these remarks: 'I am sorry if this remark caused you displeasure.'[7]

The situation in Communist East Germany, the German Democratic Republic, was quite different. There, the Nazi past was recognized, but dealt with as if the GDR had nothing to do with it. The communist state of peasants, workers and soldiers was founded on the ruins of the Third Reich, but any involvement with that past was systematically denied. It looked almost as if history had started anew on 7 October 1949, when Walter Ulbricht and Otto Grotewohl began to function as party leaders in the new Soviet-dominated state. That is also the reason why the GDR has never been involved in any kind of *Wiedergutmachung*. There was nothing to compensate, as all involvement with the Nazi past was systematically denied.

Later, after the demise of the GDR, the German situation offered another model for dealing with the past, with the opening of the Stasi (East German secret police) files. It allowed victims of the secret police to read about what had happened to them and who were the perpetrators. However, there is also a danger that individual reputations can be tarnished without due process – a danger of witch-hunting and invasion of privacy. While on the one hand, the making available of information should be judged positively, there is the danger of the improper use of such information. This is especially the case, if it is accompanied by a system of 'lustration', as in Czechoslovakia, where former government officials were denied without due process the right to serve in the government, because of their involvement in the criticized conduct of the prior regime.

INTERNATIONAL ADJUDICATION

After the international tribunals of Nuremberg and Tokyo of 1946 it took until 1993 for a decision to be reached to set up comparable tribunals: one on the former Yugoslavia, followed by that on Rwanda. Surprisingly enough, these tribunals came into being by decisions of the UN Security Council, a body whose mandate it is to look after the maintenance of international peace and security, which does not necessarily include finding ways of dealing with culprits of violations of human rights and international humanitarian law. It was mainly for political reasons that the cases of the former Yugoslavia and Rwanda were singled out for judgement. There is certainly no legal reason why human rights in these countries should be dealt with and similar events in countries such as Burundi, Cambodia, Somalia, Liberia or Zaire/ Congo (to name only a few of the more notorious ones) not. Since 1948, the International Law Commission had studied the possibility of setting up a permanent international criminal court, but it took until 1994 for the ILC to submit a full, elaborate proposal. In the summer of 1998, an international conference in Rome agreed on a draft treaty on the subject.

The decision by the Security Council determined the political character of the two tribunals. Though they are staffed by eminent jurists of a high moral character, certain decisions remain clearly outside their mandate, for political reasons. The former leader of Yugoslavia, Slobodan Milosevic who had been indicted already in 1999, was finally extradited to the Yugoslavia in June 2001. What is worse, it has so far appeared impossible to arrest two persons who have been indicted: the Serb-Bosnian leaders Radovan Karadjic and Ratko Mladic, although allied soldiers serving with the NATO forces in Serbian Bosnia encounter the two of them regularly. This brings us to the general problem of peace versus justice, which has been discussed at length in the literature.[8] There is a permanent fear that pursuit of criminal prosecutions could interfere with political agreements that were necessary to end, and keep ended both the fighting among combatants and the more numerous attacks on, and abuses of civilians. This clearly diminishes the authority of the Tribunal. If it turns out only to be able to catch the small fish, what will that mean to the cause of justice in the area? According to the Belgian sociologist Luc Huyse, the crucial challenge consists in finding a balance between the call for justice and the need for political prudence, 'or in other words, to reconcile ethical imperatives and political constraints'.[9] However, this problem has by no means been resolved. Will the pronouncements of such a tribunal be accepted? Will it, in other words, fit the sense of justice of the population concerned?

The strength of international criminal tribunals is that they help to serve to individualize guilt. However, one may pause to wonder to what extent this is indeed an advantage, if one takes Daniel Goldhagen's thesis[10] into account: he argues that most of the German people were to a greater or lesser extent involved in the extermination of the Jews. Should all Germans have been punished, then? Or only some of them? And by whom?

One may well agree with the lowest common denominator as formulated by David Forsythe:

> Perhaps the best that can be said of the Court in the light of the Dayton peace agreement is that once created the Court generated pressures that diplomats could not ignore.[11]

The establishment of the two international tribunals is in any case an institutionalized – if far from perfect – form of dealing with the past. The Yugoslavia Tribunal received a great deal of support in the Dayton Peace agreement which mentions the 'obligation of all parties to cooperate in the investigations and prosecution of war crimes and other violations of international humanitarian law'.[12] The Dayton agreement has been of great help to the operations of the Yugoslavia Tribunal. Yet, this does not mean that its problems, including the financial ones, have been solved. The best that can be said of the Rwanda Tribunal is that its progress is slow and one has to wait and see whether, and to what extent, it will have concrete results.[13]

TRUTH AND RECONCILIATION COMMISSIONS

Truth and reconciliation commissions are a relatively new phenomenon. They appear on the scene after a change of regime, when those who have been engaged in gross violations of human rights have given up their positions of power and been replaced by another, often democratic regime.

The chairman of the South African truth and reconciliation commission, Bishop Desmond Tutu, has addressed the main function of his commission as follows:

Interviewer: So how important is it that the Commission addresses these scars?
Bishop Tutu: Absolutely crucial. You see there are some people who have tried to be very facile and let bygones be bygones: they

want us to have a national amnesia. And you have to keep saying to those people that to pretend that nothing happened, to not acknowledge that something horrendous did happen to them, is to victimize the victims yet again. But even more important, experience worldwide shows that if you do not deal with a dark past such as ours, effectively look the beast in the eye, that beast is not going to lie down quietly; it is going, as sure as anything, to come back and haunt you horrendously. We are saying we need to deal with this past as quickly as possible – acknowledge that we have a disgraceful past – then close the door on it and concentrate on the present and the future.

This is the purpose of the Commission; it is just a small part of a process in which the whole nation must be engaged.[14]

Priscilla Hayner, who has done a major study on the subject, defines truth and reconciliation commissions as follows:

bodies set up to investigate a past history of human rights in a particular country – which can include violations by the military or other government forces or by armed opposition forces.[15]

The main objective of such commissions is to reveal the facts of human rights violations under the previous regime. They explicitly do not have the objective of adjudication, but of reconciliation after the facts have been revealed. The truth commissions that were set up in Chile, after the fall of the Pinochet regime, and the more recent one in South Africa have received a great deal of attention. Similar commissions have operated in Uganda, Argentina, Chad, El Salvador and the one in Guatemala that was called commission of clarification.

The composition of such commissions requires a great deal of care, in order to avoid the impression that it has been established with certain political objectives in mind or in order to whitewash the past. Its members must have the confidence of the public and their independence must be guaranteed. Independence, that is from the government. Therefore, José Zalaquett, who was a prominent member of the Chilean Commission, has argued that the commission should be financed by the state, not by the government: 'It is important that the government secures the necessary funds before the commission begins its work. It should not reserve the right to suspend funding.'[16]

Some of these commissions have considerable powers. The one in South Africa had the authority to compel witnesses to appear and to hear them under oath. It can even offer a perpetrator indemnity ('amnesty') for the human rights violations he discloses, provided he has performed them for political objectives. The Commission must decide whether the violation in question constituted such a political act.

The first and most important task of the commission is to present the true facts, or rather to recognize those facts. After all, often the true facts are already well-known among the people involved, but they ask for an official recognition. Hayner has called this 'sanctioned fact-finding'. She quotes the then director of Americas Watch, Juan Mendez: 'Knowledge that is officially sanctioned, and thereby made "part of the public cognitive scene" acquires a mysterious quality that is not there when it is "truth".'[17] The recognition of the facts should help such events from occurring again in the future. That is why the report of the Argentinian National Committee on Disappeared Persons was given the title *Nunca Más!* (Never Again!).

The assignment within the special procedure regarding missing persons in the former Yugoslavia is a special case. Part of the activities of the experts is the exhuming of mass-graves in order to be able to identify murdered persons. In Bosnia-Herzegovina, some 20 000 persons are still missing, most of them Bosnian men of Muslim origin, victims of 'ethnic cleansing' operations carried out by Serb paramilitary groups and Bosnian Serb forces. Some 5000 persons remain missing in Croatia.[18]

Would a truth commission have been a good idea for the former Yugoslavia? Michael Ignatieff, who has given careful thought to this matter, doubts this very much: 'The truth that matters to people is not factual or narrative truth but moral or interpretive truth. And this will always be an object of dispute in the Balkans.'[19] He gives the following telling example:

> Hill country Serbs in the Fora region of Bosnia told British journalists in the summer of 1992 that their ethnic militias were obliged to cleanse the area of Muslims because it was well-known fact that Muslims crucified Serbian children and floated their bodies down the river past Serbian settlements.[20]

These people will not be persuaded of the contrary by a patient assembly of facts.

Establishing a truth and reconciliation commission is not always noncontroversial. On the one hand, there are those who prefer a policy of 'forgive and forget' and who are of the opinion that this process may be harmed by the establishment of a truth and reconciliation commission. Opposite to this is the idea that true forgiveness is only possible after the recognition of the facts. Also the former perpretrators are, for obvious reasons, not very enthusiastic about the idea, unless of course it is accompanied by a process of amnesty, as in South Africa. There remains always the danger that a truth and reconciliation commission will contribute to the whitewashing of the misdeeds of a previous regime.[21]

Another question is whether, as well as members of the governing regime, the military, and the police, and members of the opposition should be called to account before a truth and reconciliation commission. In the case of South Africa, the deeds of the African National Congress (ANC) are explicitly included in the investigation. In neighbouring Namibia, the government of President Sam Nujoma has remained adamantly opposed to the whole idea of a truth and reconciliation commission. As the former leader of the South West African People's Organization (SWAPO), which was itself responsible for torture and disappearances during its fight for independence, he does not want such practices to be officially acknowledged. In contrast, in South Africa, there was a powerful political consensus, created by President Nelson Mandela, for setting up such a commission; this was obviously lacking in Namibia.

If one wants to establish such a commission, a number of questions must be answered regarding the scope of its mandate, the time-period to be covered, the question of whether its activities should be published, and the question whether the names of the culprits should be made public.[22] The question must also be answered whether it should begin its activities as soon as possible after the change of regime or whether it is wiser to have some time elapse. In favour of starting quickly is that public attention may wane after too much time has gone by. On the other hand, this may also be an argument to wait a little, so that emotions have cooled down and the commission can do its work in an atmosphere suitable for quiet and dispassionate analysis.

CONCLUSION

Human beings are able to commit all kinds of 'inhuman' acts. This observation is true for all times and all places.[23] What we like to call 'humanitarian' is a thin layer of civilization, which is ruptured time and again. The atrocities committed by the Nazis and their accomplices and the ethnic cleansing operations in the former Yugoslavia serve to demonstrate that the observation is true not only for far-away places in South America, South East Asia or Central Africa, but for the western world as well. These are violations of international rules of human rights and humanitarian law. Fortunately enough, after a longer or shorter period the violations always come to an end. Then the question must be faced: what next? How does one find a proper balance between the call for justice and political prudence? One thing is clear: most of the victims, their relatives and survivors, consider revelation of what has really happened of the utmost importance. This fact contains an assignment to society: to chart the past as well as possible and give it official recognition.

Two of the approaches discussed must, for obvious reasons, be rejected out of hand: revenge and denial of the past. Revenge is uncontrollable, violates the rule of law and holds no guarantee whatever that the guilty will be punished or the truth be revealed. The same is true of denying the past. Offering financial reparation or other forms of compensation is at least a gesture towards the victims and their relatives, and thus an official recognition of the past, which therefore is of great importance. It need not necessarily contribute toward revealing the past.

The latter objective can be served both by adjudication, either national or international or by the establishment of a truth and reconciliation commission. It is difficult to say which of these should be preferred. If adjudication according to the rules of fair trial is possible and the guilty ones can be caught and convicted, this should be preferred. But political circumstances do not always allow this procedure. In the absence of the proper preconditions for fair trial and in the absence of a permanent international tribunal, the establishment of a truth and reconciliation commission may be helpful. It should be added, however, that it remains for the time being an open question, whether finding the 'truth' will always contribute to reconciliation. Truth-finding may also reveal feelings of resentment and open old wounds. In such cases 'truth' and 'reconciliation' do not necessarily go together. However, in the end, one has to start finding the truth first and then see whether or not it will lead to reconciliation. Leaving war-crimes unpunished is worse: it leaves the cycle of impunity unbroken. The process of truth-finding and truth-telling may be as important as its actual outcome.

Truth commissions tend to emphasize the role of the victims, while criminal trials focus on the accused. The former is a quasi-judicial process, whereas the latter is a real judicial process. It may be wise not to set one's sights too high and to be satisfied with as little as one can achieve. In this context, it fits to cite Ignatieff once more; he described the potential achievements of a truth and reconciliation commission as follows:

All that a truth commission can achieve is to reduce the number of lies that can be circulated unchallenged in public discourse. [...] The past is an argument and the function of truth commissions, like the function of honest historians, is simply to purify the argument, to narrow the range of permissible lies.[24]

There is reason to be somewhat sceptical about the extent to which societies are able to learn from past experience. *Nunca Más!* is a noble objective, but it remains a question whether it can be realized and if so, for how long. The collective memory of society is short. Nevertheless, to try to reveal the truth is better than to do nothing at all.

10 Non-Governmental Organizations[1]

INTRODUCTION

Human rights organizations are part of the phenomenon known as 'non-governmental organizations' or NGOs. Curiously enough, these NGOs are defined by what they are *not*. They emphasize their distance and independence from governments, yet at the same time it is mostly the actions and activities of national governments that are the very cause and purpose of their existence. Without governments there would be no non-governmental organizations.[2] A valid description of present-day international relations should, in addition to taking note of the continued role of nation-states and of intergovernmental organizations, pay due attention to the role and function of non-governmental organizations. That seems to be no less true of the sector of international relations that deals with human rights. The World Conference on Human Rights, held in Vienna in 1993, brought together approximately 10 000 persons, including 3000 delegates from NGOs.[3]

Non-governmental human rights organizations exist in great numbers and have developed a great number of activities. However, relatively little is known about their effectiveness or impact, except for the fact that they tend to rely on what is commonly known as the 'mobilization of shame'. Yet it is hard to put a finger on what exactly constitutes such mobilization. In this chapter, an effort is made to analyse conditions of effectiveness of internationally operating human rights non-governmental organizations. After a brief look at problems of definition, the following subjects are dealt with: reliability, the problem of access versus independence, representativeness, mutual cooperation, media-attention and timing.

DEFINITION

Non-governmental human rights organizations (HRNGOs) exist in all sizes and shapes. They may run from a letter-head 'organization' basically existing of one individual with or without expert knowledge of the subject, to large organizations with thousands of members. The only thing these phenomena have in common is that they are, or claim to be, 'non-governmental'. The addition of 'claim to be' is needed, to cover the so-called 'GONGOs', 'QUANGOs' and 'DONGOs' referred to by Gordenker and Weiss, which look like HRNGOs, but are not truly non-governmental.[4] It is not always easy to distinguish in practice these government-supported organizations from the real thing. Apparently, governments find it useful to hide some of their activities under the guise of being 'non-governmental', presumably because that title adds to their effectiveness. Other NGOs are usually in the best position to tell whether any group, old or newly established, should be considered a true member of the club.

The Canadian human rights expert Laurie Wiseberg has developed the following definition of a non-governmental human rights organiza-tion: 'a private organization which devotes significant resources to the promotion and protection of human rights, which is independent of both governmental and political groups that seek direct political power, and which itself does not seek such power'.[5] She thus clearly distin-guishes NGOs from political parties that are also private associations but which do seek to achieve political power. NGOs are, as Gordenker and Weiss have succinctly put it, 'private in their form, but public in their purpose'.[6] This definition covers HRNGOs of many different types and sizes, large and small, well-endowed and poor, professional and less professional. At the UN World Conference on Human Rights in 1993, differences of view arose between large, well-organized NGOs, usually based in western countries, on the one hand, and relatively poor, less well-organized organizations often from 'Southern' coun-tries, on the other. The latter showed some irritation that the former assumed that they could speak on behalf of *all* NGOs.[7] The claim of dif-ferent 'cultural' approaches, as well as different interests, does not seem to be limited to governments alone.[8] The difficulty of reaching a more or less permanent form of cooperation among HRNGOs may be partly caused by this lack of agreement. However, little study has been devoted so far to North–South tensions among HRNGOs.

RELIABILITY

Providing reliable information (to governments, intergovernmental organizations, politicians, the news media, academics as well as the general public) is the most important precondition to be fulfilled for any NGO to have an impact. It is probably much more important than the views and comments that are being expressed, as these are often already known anyway. Information that is trustworthy is eagerly sought by all concerned.

Members of UN supervisory committees make increasing use of information supplied to them by NGOs for the purpose of the examination of state reports. In the early years, the use of such 'unofficial information' was frowned upon. For instance, especially Eastern European members of the UN Human Rights Committee felt that the Committee should not use such information.[9] Members of the Committee would surreptitiously glance at documents submitted to them by NGOs, hiding them under their desks. Nowadays, however, the use of this type of information is no longer subject to debate within the Committee.[10] Indeed, members of this as well as other UN expert committees eagerly look for NGO materials before a country examination, 'because it helps make their questioning more precise, factual and less abstract'.[11] The thematic mechanisms of the UN rely almost exclusively upon NGO information. No less than 74 per cent of the cases taken up by the UN Working Group on Arbitrary Detentions in 1994 were brought by international NGOs; another 23 per cent came from national NGOs, and 3 per cent from families.[12]

It is in the area of the collection of sound, reliable information that the need for a professional expert staff is most clearly felt. NGOs that command such a staff can more easily provide such information than organizations that have to rely mostly on the activities of volunteers. Volunteers may also possess the necessary expertise, but often lack the collective memory of the past. A body of information is usually built on previous knowledge as well as personal acquaintances. Volunteers come and go and, though mostly highly motivated, they may lack experience. Therefore, the existence of a professional staff may greatly add to the information-gathering role of the NGO. Amnesty International, with a professional staff of almost 300 individuals in its International Secretariat in London – which is more than the entire staff of the Office of the UN High Commissioner for Human Rights in Geneva – is an example of such an organization. Other well-known organizations are the International Commission of Jurists, the 'watch' committees in the United States, and Article XIX, which works for freedom of expression all over the world.

Reliability is closely linked to credibility. A government that is the target of such information will do its utmost to discredit such an organization by questioning its motives (for instance attempting to dismiss them as 'political'), its financial resources ('CIA-supported', 'communist umbrella organization', etc.) and also its methods of work.[13] In case such efforts are successful and the credibility of the organization's work has been successfully challenged, its impact may suffer for many years to come. An example outside the field of human rights is the environmental protection organization Greenpeace, whose credibility seems to have suffered from the information it provided on the dismantling of the oil-platform *Brent Spar* in 1995, which was proved to have been at best only partially correct.

'New' kinds of violations of human rights seem to occur all the time. Before the seventies, most people thought that torture was a matter of the past. Human rights organizations have brought out the fact that torture belongs very much to this day and age. The phenomenon of involuntary disappearances was another such phenomenon brought to light by NGOs. In the nineties, the world was confronted with 'ethnic cleansing', of which nobody had heard before. The hearings before the Yugoslavia Tribunal in The Hague provide almost daily new material of what human beings can do to each other. Reports about Rwanda, Burundi, Congo and Kosovo provide us with new material about human atrocities. Moreover, NGOs can provide new insights or new perspectives which create renewed public interest for what are in reality ancient problems.

ACCESS VERSUS INDEPENDENCE

For an NGO it is important to have access to the government. This means that it should be able to approach government officials to make them aware of its views. 'Access' may mean many things. It may mean that the organization can call an official on the telephone to make him or her aware of new information which may then be put to him/her in written form. It may mean having the ability to engage the official in a formal or informal conversation with representatives of the NGO, in order to raise the matter at the ministerial or cabinet level or at intergovernmental meetings. The degree of such access may differ according to the role human rights play on the domestic political scene of the country in question. In politically open societies, such as the Netherlands or Norway, access is easier and more effective than in China or Nigeria, where it may not exist at all.

In certain countries, former NGO executives hold positions in national governments and NGO representatives are routinely included in official delegations to sessions of the General Assembly of the United Nations and special conferences. Antonio Donini, himself a senior officer in the Executive Office of the UN Secretary-General, considers this development 'a welcome feature'.[14] And so it is, if seen from the perspective of gaining maximum access. We should, however, pause for a moment and reflect on the possible repercussions for the independent position of NGOs. Maximum access may be gained at the expense of risking one's independence. When, for example, the Netherlands Government invited two NGO members to participate in its official delegation to the Vienna World Conference on Human Rights, these two persons were given maximum access. At the same time, they were expected to share some of the workload with the other members of the delegation, such as writing the daily reports to the ministry in The Hague, which for all practical purposes was hard for them to refuse. Yet, an outside observer may wonder, whether when doing this they were not in danger of losing their independent position by having become more or less 'ordinary' members of the delegation.

Australia provides another vivid example. There, members of parliament, including members of the government, serve on a committee, 'Parliamentarians for Amnesty International'. Without questioning the motives and good intentions of these individuals, one may wonder about the wisdom of this practice. The distinction between what is the government and what is an NGO may thus be blurred. Yet, that distinction remains important, because the government can never go as far as an NGO in embracing human rights. A government has by definition other concerns. Therefore, there should always remain a clear distinction between what is government and what is not.[15] If an NGO succeeds in penetrating into the innermost chambers of governmental deliberations, it may end up by having to share some of the government's political responsibilities as well.

Herman Burgers, who himself has served in a senior position within the Dutch Ministry of Foreign Affairs and after his retirement became a member of the governing board of the Dutch section of Amnesty International, relates the activities of an official of the Ministry *who at the same time* worked on behalf of Amnesty International: 'In this setting it is remarkable to note that no one seems to object to civil servants, in the capacity of members and chairman of an Amnesty International Committee, criticizing the policy of their own ministry. Dutch NGOs indeed play a peculiar role.'[16] In fact, the ministry may be less troubled by such mixing of responsibilities than the NGO that would seem to benefit from the arrangement.

Some governments make a considerable effort to maintain periodic contacts with NGOs in the field of human rights. For example, the

Canadian Ministry of Foreign Affairs organizes once a year a two-day consultation with NGOs. These meetings precede the principal meetings of the UN Commission on Human Rights. The meetings which may include as many as 60 to 80 participants, are addressed by the Foreign Minister or his deputy. This 'forum' is a useful meeting, though it has also been described as 'a dialogue of the deaf'.[17] This procedure provides the NGOs with at least access to the responsible ministry officials, although it does of course not guarantee them that their views will be adopted. NGO representatives sometimes tend to forget that access is a necessary but not a sufficient condition for success. Apparently, the invitations to these meetings are widely distributed and no NGOs have so far been refused access to these meetings.

Weiss and Gordenker have called attention to a less formalized, though perhaps even more effective channel of access, either direct or indirect, which consists of prominent persons, who thanks to their expertise, experience, office or other distinguishing characteristic earn respect or deference.[18] Examples that come to mind are former US President Jimmy Carter, the late Eleanor Roosevelt, the late Willy Brandt, former Norwegian Prime Minister Gro Harlem Brundlandt and former Dutch Foreign Minister Peter Kooijmans. No less important than knowledge and expertise may be the personal acquaintances such persons may have. As the old Dutch saying goes: 'Kennis is macht, maar kennissen geven nog meer macht.'[19]

It should be clear then that access to the government is of extremely great importance to NGOs. No impact without access; though access is no guarantee for success. NGOs should at the same time be aware of the dangers too easy access may entail. They may be hedged in by the government and its permanent officials, thus running the risk of being seen by the public as an extension of the government. For a government, it is of great importance to maintain close relations with NGOs it considers reliable. Seen from the government's perspective, there is little to be lost and much to be gained by such close relations. It is rather the NGOs that have to maintain a certain measure of caution in these relations.

REPRESENTATIVENESS

Non-governmental organizations are often referred to as 'grass roots organizations' which term suggests that they are closer to ordinary people than, for instance, government officials. Otto has referred to what has been coined the 'Third System': 'my interest is in those non-state entities that are speaking for groups and individuals who do not believe that states are adequately representing their interests'.[20] The extent to which that picture is correct depends on the question whether an NGO has a membership and how the structure of the group is organized. Non-membership organizations such as the Human Rights Watch organizations in the United States, may on the whole be able to react quicker and be more flexible in their approaches to governments than membership organizations. Yet, the impact of a membership organization may be greater, because governments are aware that the views expressed by such an NGO are not only those of a small group of experts, but may also reflect those of a larger constitution. If the membership is relatively large, as in the case of Amnesty International,[21] politicians may pay extra attention to the NGO's views, because of possible electoral consequences. Another advantage of membership organizations is that the leadership is accountable to the rank and file, which means that the membership may exert some kind of control over the actions of the leadership. Fowler has referred, however, to the danger of 'grass-roots apathy' – NGOs that become so much involved in participating in international and national debates that they lose sight of their goals of empowerment.[22]

The Economic and Social Council of the United Nations, in its 1996 session, decided on new 'Arrangements for Consultation with Non-Governmental Organizations'.[23] One of the principles to be applied in establishing consultative relations with NGOs is that the organization should have 'a representative structure and possess appropriate mechanisms of accountability to its members, who shall exercise effective control over its policies and actions through the exercise of voting rights or other appropriate democratic and transparent decision-making processes'.[24] Criteria for judging such representativeness were, however, not spelled out.

The mere fact that an NGO has a membership does not necessarily mean that the group is democratically organized. As Gordenker and Weiss have pointed out: 'The nature of representation within nongovernmental organizations as well as within their coalitions, and by NGOs within international gatherings, is a source of some perplexity if not ambiguity for analysts.'[25] The two authors suggest moreover that NGO leaders may push their own personal agendas rather than those of their constituents.[26] Internationally, there is a difference between 'top-down' and 'bottom-up' organizations. The former are centrally organized international groups with national sections, while the latter are federations of nationally organized groups. Both kinds may be more or less democratically organized.

Some of the problems that may arise when organizing an international-membership NGO on a democratic basis are well illustrated by the example of Amnesty International. This organization is based on a worldwide voluntary membership, which consists of sections, affiliated groups and individual members.[27] The authority for the conduct of affairs is vested in the International Council, which meets once very two years. Only representatives of national sections have the right to vote. All national sections hold at least one vote in the International Council. However, sections receive additional votes in proportion to the number of Amnesty groups or individual members they hold. Thus the larger sections, which also hold the purse strings within the organization, such as those of the United States, the United Kingdom, Sweden, France, Germany and the Netherlands, are entitled to additional representatives which may add up to as many as six votes per national delegation.[28] The result is that in the International Council the Netherlands, for example, rates as a major power – a striking experience for those Amnesty representatives that are familiar with similar meetings at the governmental level. Smaller sections have repeatedly tried to change this system of weighted voting into one on a 'one-section-one-vote' basis, so far, however, without any success. Whether the existing system should be seen as democratic, is a matter of debate. A system whereby each national delegation is accorded one vote, as in the General Assembly of the United Nations, is not necessarily more democratic than a system of weighted voting. In the latter, the individual members or groups are more strongly represented. A side-effect is that, within the Amnesty International Council, the larger as well as wealthier sections of the 'North' can easily outvote the sections of the 'South'. This was, for instance, crucial in the 1991 decision of the Council that Amnesty International should work on behalf of imprisoned homosexuals – an issue which was strongly opposed by Asian and African sections.[29]

In discussing the desirability of 'international participatory democracy' Otto has called for the need for a form of accountability of NGOs to their constituencies in civil society.[30] She rightly makes the point that international NGOs need to evolve an infrastructure which would assist with such projects. She mentions as two key aims of NGO participatory strategies 'to build in protections against Western domination and to promote the strengthening of transnational identities'.[31] However, she fails to acknowledge that the 'Western dominated' NGOs may be among the more effective ones. Building protection against such western domination may go at the expense of the very NGOs that work on behalf of the weak and downtrodden. It is also by no means an established fact that improving the democratic nature of membership organizations will be to the benefit of those on whose behalf the NGOs are working.

The issue of whom precisely NGOs represent remains unresolved for the time being. In view of all of these difficulties, one may well come to the conclusion that the issues the NGOs take up are more important than their own democratic representativeness. But in the absence of more formal criteria for such representation, the claims of many of them to be grass-roots movements should be taken with a grain of salt.

COOPERATION AMONG NGOs

NGOs are notorious for their wish for independence. Coordinating NGOs is, according to one UN official, 'like herding cats'.[32] This, it may be added by way of comment, is equally true of governments. Among NGOs, Amnesty International has traditionally stood out for its independence and unwillingness to associate itself with other HRNGOs for fear of endangering its cherished limited mandate. On the other hand, NGOs are aware of the need to work together to realize common aims. Ritchie mentions a great number of examples of successful cooperation between NGO coalitions and UN agencies: 'NGO coalitions are perhaps increasingly essential partners in the advocacy roles that are needed to ensure that governments make decisions in the global public interest and carry out the obligations that result from international conferences and conventions.'[33]

Paradoxically, international conferences organized by *governments* to discuss pressing international problems serve as a catalyst for bringing together non-governmental organizations. Recent examples are the world conferences on environment and development (Rio de Janeiro 1992), human rights (Vienna 1993), population and development (Cairo 1994), women's issues (Beijing 1995), housing problems (Istanbul 1996), and the environment (Kyoto 1997), all of which saw the phenomenon of 'parallel' conferences of NGOs.[34] These NGOs might never have met, had not the governmental meetings brought them together. Ritchie even claims that the success of the intergovernmental meeting itself depends to a great extent on the activities of the NGOs: 'World conferences and summits need the full-scale input and presence of NGOs and their coalitions to have any hope of achieving their goals.'[35]

The World Conference on Human Rights in 1993 in Vienna witnessed an impressive gathering of more than 1500 NGOs, whose meetings 'downstairs' in the Austria Centre were far more colourful and
more informative than the somewhat dull meetings of government representatives 'upstairs'.[36] Prior to the World Conference, human rights
NGOs met in order to discuss the accomplishments and shortcomings
of the UN human rights programme and to formulate common recommendations to be considered by the governments at the official conference. The NGO Forum was addressed by a number of well-known
keynote speakers.[37] Many of the organizations represented in Vienna,
such as representatives of Kurdish, Palestinian, Basque, Sendero Lumi-
noso ('Shining Path') and other armed opposition groups, all of whom
clearly aim for political power, are not *human rights* NGOs in the sense
of Wiseberg's definition quoted at the beginning of this chapter. That
was also true of the representatives of the Christian Democratic and
Liberal International, both of whom have close ties with political parties of the same name. Clearly, not very strict rules for admission had
been applied. In view of the diverse nature of the various NGOs attending the conference, it is hardly surprising that 'clashes ensued between
the new, national NGOs and traditional international NGOs'.[38]

After the Vienna Conference, cooperation among HRNGOs was
expected henceforth to be coordinated by an NGO Liaison Committee
(NLC), which was elected on the last day of the NGO Forum.[39] The
intention was to give this NLC a permanent character. However, this
did not work out and the committee was formally disbanded in 1995.
The reason was that the regional networks – in Asia, Africa and Latin
America – felt that it was more important to work at the regional level
than to try to work internationally.[40]

There exists considerable pressure, both from the outside and the
inside, on HRNGOs to coordinate their efforts. From the outside,
certain governments try to limit the number of NGO interventions
in intergovernmental meetings, using the argument that it is too time-
consuming to have to listen to the statements of so many NGOs,
which basically have one and the same message to convey.[41] These same
governments have no qualms about similar endless interventions by
diplomatic delegates, exercising their 'right of reply', etc. The NGOs
should show more self-discipline by grouping their statements.[42] The
Principles for Consultation with Non-Governmental Organizations,
adopted by the ECOSOC, contain a similar suggestion: 'Where there
exist a number of organizations with similar objectives, interests and
basic views in a given field, they may, for the purposes of consultation

with the Council, form a joint committee or other body authorized to carry on such consultation for the group as a whole.'[43]

In principle, the NGOs themselves also see the need for closer cooperation and coordination of their activities, in order to mobilize scarce resources and avoid duplication of efforts. However, in view of the diverse nature of the various NGOs, with regard to aims to be achieved, their size, financial resources and cultural background, it has so far proved extremely difficult to bring about such cooperation. The independent International Service for Human Rights, a shoestring operation in Geneva, is doing its best to supply information – e.g. on procedures at the UN, schedules of meetings, the nature of the issues under discussion, etc. – to all human rights organizations. This type of effort clearly deserves to be expanded. As soon as the provision of facilities in conference centres and the right to take the floor at intergovernmental gatherings, let alone the provision of financial aid, are at stake, NGOs ostensibly working for similar aims tend to become fierce competitors. In this respect, they resemble competing governments who also are reluctant to give up their sovereign rights for the sake of mutual cooperation. One thing is clear, however: it should be left to the NGOs themselves to find the proper channels for cooperation. It is NGOs who should themselves find the ways to organize their own international cooperation.

MEDIA ATTENTION

HRNGOs would be hard put to have any impact, if the media did not pay attention to their activities. The voluminous *Yearbooks* of Amnesty International and other human rights organizations may be reliable and trustworthy, but they are rarely read by government officials or the general public in their entirety. Their message is normally conveyed by accounts in the newspapers, radio and television. NGO activities at the Vienna World Conference were given more space in the media than the official conference.[44]

The need for publicity may lead NGOs to what Ritchie has called 'dramatic postures' for the sake of gaining publicity.[45] Such stunts may include pop-music performances by well-known entertainers, television shows (on occasion sponsored by commercial firms), or imitations of human rights violations such as torture or isolated imprisonment. The limits of what is acceptable in this sphere and the ethics of accepting company money for such purposes are often hotly debated within the organizations.

There is always a danger that the message the human rights organization wants to convey may be lost in the glare of publicity, that, as it were, 'the show takes over'. For instance, many members of the audiences attending the pop concerts in a world tour by such artists as Bruce Springsteen, Peter Gabriel and Sting, in the 'Human Rights Now!' event in 1988 may not have been aware that they were taking part in an *awareness event.* [46] The tour was underwritten by a commercial enterprise. [47] Internally, within Amnesty there was initially a great deal of discussion over the wisdom of having such an arrangement. In the event, the commercial enterprise was given a relatively low profile during the concerts, thanks to which fears that Amnesty might be associated with the selling of one particular brand of sports wear, did not materialize.

The 'mobilization of shame' is greatly dependent on media exposure. Politicians in general and governments in particular are more likely to be persuaded to act on behalf of human rights in the face of media attention or the threat of it. Even if HRNGOs make use of 'silent diplomacy' when approaching governments, for instance to bring about the release of a particular political prisoner or to end cases of torture, there is always the threat of media exposure around the corner. What remains in the last resort is publicity in order to try to change a government's attitude and behaviour by public pressure. Chances of success are greater if the country concerned traditionally pays attention to expressions of public opinion, but there are no governments – ranging from full-fledged democracies to dictatorships – that can afford to ignore fully their public relations. In addition, public exposure may also lead to the exertion of external pressure by other governments or intergovernmental organizations.

TIMING

Timing is essential for impact. An action that comes too early may be as ineffective as one that comes too late. Therefore it is of crucial importance that an NGO is well-informed about the precise nature and the stages of the decision-making process, both as far as governmental and intergovernmental agencies are concerned. Agendas may be set or changed at the last moment. Informal consultations may take place that are crucial to the decision-making process. International meetings are always short of time, which may lead to last-minute decisions. At international conferences, the preparatory process may be as important as, or even more important than the actual conference itself, which may last only for one or two weeks.[48] Representatives of HRNGOs must always be well aware of such factors and be prepared to strike when the iron is hot.

National governments may also be engaged in the manipulation of time. Faced with situations where all available choices have negative repercussions, a government may opt for postponing the decision, hoping for a change of circumstances. Gaining time may be akin to victory. The government may also suggest that nothing has been decided yet, leaving open when exactly a definitive decision will be taken.

For the purpose of being well aware of the timing process, it is helpful to have permanent representations in national capitals and at the headquarters of intergovernmental organizations. Amnesty International, for example, maintains permanent missions at the United Nations in New York and Geneva and with the European Union in Brussels.

CONCLUSIONS

In this chapter emphasis has been put on the role of international human rights NGOs. It must be noted that in addition there are important other roles for NGOs such as awareness-raising through human rights education, standard-setting, extension of supervisory mechanisms and the necessary follow-up. Human rights NGOs play a role of some significance in international relations. That in itself remains a remarkable feat that calls for explanation. They criticize governments for violating human rights or for allowing or condoning such acts. Why should national governments pay attention to what HRNGOs have to say? The NGOs have no power; they rely on a relatively limited membership, if at all. They pose no economic or military threat. Yet they are given the floor in meetings of intergovernmental organizations and in international conferences. Their representatives are received in national capitals and their views are paid at least lip-service. Governments even go as far as setting up or sponsoring fake NGOs to counter the activities of the real ones. Why?

The only answer to this question,[49] which is the one that is offered by the NGOs themselves, is the often cited 'mobilization of shame'. This refers to the circumstance that all governments like to be known as civilized and as observing the international human rights standards which they themselves have helped to devise. No government will easily admit that it allows violations of those standards to take place. Yet most governments in the world at some time or other violate them. This discrepancy between norm and practice creates the space in which HRNGOs can operate. Starting from the point of agreement as to how governments ought to behave, they draw attention to violations of these standards. Basically, governments have two ways of reacting to such allegations: admittance or denial. In view of their above-cited adherence to international human rights standards, admittance of violations of such standards logically means that something will be done about it. In such cases, one can say that the NGO's activities have been successful.

If, as often happens, the government in question denies the allegation, the reputation of the NGO for reliability is at stake. In the absence of other elements of power, reliability is the only source of strength HRNGOs can dispose of. By continuous truthful reporting an organization can build up a reputation of reliability, which must be jealously guarded. It can be threatened from two sides. First, of course, by an offending government which may try either to discredit the HRNGO by questioning its motives or methods of work and by disseminating disinformation. But there is also a danger from the opposite direction. Political opponents of the government in question may try to use HRNGOs for purposes of their own by feeding the HRNGO with news about alleged atrocities on the part of the government which may actually never have taken place.

Conditions for reliable reporting are a well-trained professional staff, access to information and of course the necessary financial resources. The latter are needed for paying the staff, building up a database, financing on-site inspections and to pay for the publications of the organization.

Reliability is a precondition, but not a guarantee of success. That depends also on the degree of access to government officials and the help of the media. As has been pointed out in this chapter, access to government officials is tremendously important to HRNGOs, yet should not be gained at the risk of losing independence. Access is a two-way process. It allows HRNGOs to put their views to government officials, but these officials in turn will, of course, also use the opportunity to try to influence the NGOs. There is admittedly a thin line between having access and guarding the independent position of an NGO, in order to show that it is not working to advance a particular government's interests. By their nature, NGOs can afford to be more single-minded in pressing human rights issues than governments. A government has other matters of concern as well. That is why it is to be recommended that there should always remain some distance between the two.

Again, access alone is no guarantee for success. An HRNGO that commands a membership can use that membership for various purposes, such as letter-writing to cabinet ministers, government officials and members of parliament of its own or of foreign countries. The membership – if sufficiently large – may also serve as an electoral threat. It comes close to what may be seen as an element of public opinion in the field of human rights. However that may be, the issue of representativeness of HRNGOs remains in the end an unresolved matter. There is no way of setting rules in this regard. In the end, it is left to the HRNGOs themselves to decide on their own representativeness.

Coordination at least, and mutual cooperation if possible, are helpful for HRNGOs. They may decide to channel their efforts and thus be more effective. Yet such coordination and cooperation must not be the result only of government prodding. Governments may find NGOs troublesome and try to limit their activities by calling for 'restraint' and 'self-discipline', however reluctant they may be to display such restraint and self-discipline themselves. NGOs should opt for coordination and cooperation only if they find this helpful to carry out their activities. Such cooperation may be found in the realm of exchange of information and pooling of efforts. On the other hand, the existence of some form of healthy competition among NGOs is not necessarily a bad thing. It may actually be helpful to the cause of human rights and to the plight of victims of human rights violations.

Little has to be added to what has already been said in this chapter about the importance of media attention. It is a crucial condition for impact by HRNGOs. Without media attention, no impact. Indeed, the mobilization of shame can only be realized if the communication media pay attention to what the HRNGOs have to say. Publicity is needed in order to seek public pressure to effect governments' attitudes and behaviour. However, NGOs should be careful with pulling stunts just for the sake of media attention. Such stunts may be counterproductive if they become ends in themselves. Repeating the same message over and over may not be in accordance with standard practices for getting media attention. Yet, through the occurrence of continually 'new' forms of violations, the media are bound to retain an interest in the subject.

Finally, HRNGOs must keep the time factor in mind. Information about the nature of the decision-making process is important to choose the right time for actions. Correct timing can be a decisive factor for achieving maximum impact. Experience with the way governments and intergovernmental agencies operate can be helpful in this regard. Here,

HRNGOs may help each other by exchanging information. Also, former or present government officials may be willing to share their experience and expertise in this field.

All of the factors discussed in this chapter contribute to the effectiveness of HRNGOs. All of them are necessary, yet none of them on its own will be sufficient. In the end it all depends on the 'conscience of mankind' mentioned in the Universal Declaration of Human Rights. The mobilization of this conscience – and shaming governments into respecting human rights – are the only and most effective weapons of non-governmental organizations working in the field of human rights.[50]

11 Concluding Observations

The tenth of December 1998 was the fiftieth anniversary of the Universal Declaration of Human Rights. That is no cause for celebration, but rather for reflection. That reflection should concern the fact that so few aspects of the rights mentioned in the Declaration have been realized. Genocide, 'ethnic cleansing', disappearances, torture and extrajudicial executions belong in many countries as the order of the day. One may think of such places as Rwanda, Burundi, Congo, Nigeria, Algeria, Sri Lanka, Colombia, and Kosovo – to name only a few of the worst cases. Of the economic, social and cultural rights even less has been realized, as the situation in such countries as Haiti, Nepal, Cambodia, Yemen, Ethiopia and most of the other African countries has shown. For the people living in those countries the realization of universal human rights is still a very distant ideal.

At the same time, much discussion is taking place in Geneva and New York, where national delegates meet, in order to exchange views and to take decisions. Solemn conferences are held, where resolutions and recommendations are adopted and sent to the national capitals. There are endless deliberations about the small print of international treaties and declarations on human rights. Representatives of non-governmental organizations play their part in this international circuit. Even assuming the good intentions of the diplomats concerned, there is a grave danger that all those international meetings are very distant from the ordinary people. International conferences, such as the world conferences on human rights in Teheran (1968) and in Vienna (1993) are worthwhile endeavours, as long as the people whose rights are at stake are not left out of sight. Here lies an important role for the High Commissioner for Human Rights. He or she can develop into a kind of 'conscience of mankind', asking continually for attention to violations of and threats to human rights all over the world. The first High Commissioner, José Ayalo Lasso, was too much of a traditional diplomat to play this role. His successor, the former Irish President Mary Robinson, was more inclined to do it. She developed into a kind of international 'Ombudswoman for human rights', having the 'mobilization of shame' as her daily assignment.[1] She should not only aim for the small and less influential states, but also pay attention to the great powers and pay equal attention to economic, social, and cultural rights as to civil and political rights.

The High Commissioner needs the support of 'like-minded' states willing to work on behalf of human rights. Non-governmental organizations remain indispensable, both for calling permanent attention to a subject that governments might be tempted to 'forget', and for supplying information. It would be a good thing, besides existing NGOs that try to promote civil and political rights, if more organizations of comparable strength and impact were to deal with economic, social and cultural rights. Cooperation by the press and the other media is likewise indispensable. Without media-coverage only a few of the NGO messages would reach the public, but the press also has a role of its own to play in the promotion of human rights. It is to a large extent thanks to the media that human rights have found a place on the political agenda.

In the remainder of this chapter we will discuss six controversial themes that are at issue in current debates about human rights. Most of these have been touched upon directly or indirectly in the previous chapters.

In the first place there is the continuing debate about the issue of the universality of human rights. That debate has an empirical as well a strongly emotional and normative character. The empirical aspect calls for research into the extent to which internationally agreed standards, as contained in the Universal Declaration and other human rights mechanisms, are in fact accepted all over the world and, to the extent that this is not the case, what are the exact differences that can be observed. That means interdisciplinary research by sociologists, cultural anthropologists, lawyers, political scientists, economists, and historians from the West as well the rest of the world. Only then will it be possible to determine whether there is indeed an 'emerging consensus', as has been suggested earlier in this book.

At the same time, there is also a normative question to be answered: *should* human rights be accepted everywhere? From the foregoing it should be clear that the present author happens to think so. This does of course not mean that these norms should be imposed on people who happen to think differently. It does mean, however, that permanent pressure should be exercised on states to implement internationally agreed standards. That demands continuous improvement of global and regional instruments of supervision. In regard to the latter, it would be of great importance, if apart from the existing supervision mechanisms for Europe, the Americas, and Africa, a regional supervision mechanism were to be developed for Asia or parts of Asia, and the Pacific as well. Experiences with such mechanisms in Europe and the Americas show that regional systems do not detract from the global supervision mechanisms of the United Nations; they rather supplement them.

Much has already been said about the promotion of economic, social and cultural rights, as well as civil and political rights. Next to reasons of a substantive nature, there is also a tactical consideration why western governments should insist on the promotion of economic, social and cultural rights. It would give them a strong argument in the dialogue with those non-western states, such as China, Singapore and Malaysia, who claim that western countries are mainly working for the promotion of their own (economic) interests. Western states should demonstrate that they are serious about the promotion of *all* human rights, as mentioned in the Final Declaration of the 1993 World Conference on Human Rights in Vienna.

A third important issue concerns the place of collective human rights. It should by now be clear that the promotion of individual human rights alone is not enough. There are quite a few unjust situations in the world which can only be solved by granting rights to collectivities. One may think of the right to development, the right of self-determination, the right to a clean natural environment, and the right to be free from genocide. It has been shown above that granting such rights should not be at the expense of individual rights. There is also a tactical aspect to consider. Western countries would do well to set aside their present reluctance in this area. In the dialogue with non-western states they might thus gain in persuasiveness.

The debate about how to deal with past violations of human rights and humanitarian law is speeding up. The Yugoslavia Tribunal appears to achieve more than many had thought at first. Perhaps this will also be the case with the Rwanda Tribunal. Much progress has been made with the realization of a Permanent International Criminal Court. The situation in this field seems to be a little more hopeful than a few years ago, when not much was happening. The so-called truth and reconciliation commissions are a new phenomenon which, in a number of countries, have made it possible to call those guilty of human rights violations to account. This is of great importance to the victims and their relatives.

In the fifth place, large multinational enterprises are coming to realize that they also have to fulfil a role in helping to guard the observance of human rights in countries where they are located.[2] No longer do they only refer to 'observing the laws of the land' when being confronted with human rights violations of whatever kind. Non-governmental organizations have begun a dialogue with them, to consider in which way multinationals can fulfil their responsibilities. This type of dialogue should be continued and, where necessary be stimulated and encouraged by governments. This may also be a task for the High Commissioner for Human Rights.

Finally, there are the refugees and displaced persons whose fate is indissolubly linked to violations of human rights in their countries of origin. In this field, very little has been achieved so far by the international community. The UN High Commissioner for Refugees is among one of the more effective UN organs, but fails nevertheless in the care for refugees and displaced persons. The latter category in particular is on the increase.[3] The Western European states no longer practice what used to be called a 'generous' policy of admittance. On the contrary, they are inclined to close their borders. The Schengen agreement has opened internal borders within Europe, but externally the opposite is true. Official policy leads to degrading situations, which stand in sharp contrast to the principles contained in the Universal Declaration of Human Rights. Here lies an important task for all those who are concerned with principles such as human dignity and equal treatment, to persuade people in the receiving countries, the parliaments and in the end also the governments, that the acceptance of human rights should have consequences for a more generous policy of admittance. It would be a step in the right direction if the UN High Commissioner for Refugees were to be provided with greater financial means to take care of a more dignified treatment of all refugees and displaced persons.

Concern for human rights is permanent in nature. I once observed that nobody ever does enough on behalf of human rights. That is true for governments, for intergovernmental organizations, for national parliaments, for non-governmental organizations and for private individuals. It is praiseworthy if human rights are accepted in principle, but that is nowhere near enough. The implementation of these principles should be permanently watched. That should be everybody's task.

Appendix: Universal Declaration of Human Rights

Adopted and proclaimed by General Assembly resolution 217 A (III) of 10 December 1948

Preamble

Whereas recognition of the inherent dignity and of the equal and inalienable rights of all members of the human family is the foundation of freedom, justice and peace in the world,

Whereas disregard and contempt for human rights have resulted in barbarous acts which have outraged the conscience of mankind, and the advent of a world in which human beings shall enjoy freedom of speech and belief and freedom from fear and want has been proclaimed as the highest aspiration of the common people,

Whereas it is essential, if man is not to be compelled to have recourse, as a last resort, to rebellion against tyranny and oppression, that human rights should be protected by the rule of law,

Whereas it is essential to promote the development of friendly relations between nations,

Whereas the peoples of the United Nations have in the Charter reaffirmed their faith in fundamental human rights, in the dignity and worth of the human person and in the equal rights of men and women and have determined to promote social progress and better standards of life in larger freedom,

Whereas Member States have pledged themselves to achieve, in cooperation with the United Nations, the promotion of universal respect for and observance of human rights and fundamental freedoms,

Whereas a common understanding of these rights and freedoms is of the greatest importance for the full realization of this pledge,

Now, therefore,

The General Assembly,

Proclaims this Universal Declaration of Human Rights as a common standard of achievement for all peoples and all nations, to the end that every individual and every organ of society, keeping this Declaration constantly in mind, shall strive by teaching and education to promote respect for these rights and freedoms and by progressive measures, national and international, to secure their universal and effective recognition and observance, both among the peoples of Member States themselves and among the peoples of territories under their jurisdiction.

Article 1
All human beings are born free and equal in dignity and rights. They are endowed with reason and conscience and should act towards one another in a spirit of brotherhood.

Article 2
Everyone is entitled to all the rights and freedoms set forth in this Declaration, without distinction of any kind, such as race, colour, sex, language, religion, political or other opinion, national or social origin, property, birth or other status.

Furthermore, no distinction shall be made on the basis of the political, jurisdictional or international status of the country or territory to which a person belongs, whether it be independent, trust, non-self-governing or under any other limitation of sovereignty.

Article 3
Everyone has the right to life, liberty and security of person.

Article 4
No one shall be held in slavery or servitude; slavery and the slave trade shall be prohibited in all their forms.

Article 5
No one shall be subjected to torture or to cruel, inhuman or degrading treatment or punishment.

Article 6
Everyone has the right to recognition everywhere as a person before the law.

Article 7
All are equal before the law and are entitled without any discrimination to equal protection of the law. All are entitled to equal protection against any discrimination in violation of this Declaration and against any incitement to such discrimination.

Article 8
Everyone has the right to an effective remedy by the competent national tribunals for acts violating the fundamental rights granted him by the constitution or by law.

Article 9
No one shall be subjected to arbitrary arrest, detention or exile.

Article 10
Everyone is entitled in full equality to a fair and public hearing by an independent and impartial tribunal, in the determination of his rights and obligations and of any criminal charge against him.

Article 11
Everyone charged with a penal offence has the right to be presumed innocent until proved guilty according to law in a public trial at which he has had all the guarantees necessary for his defence.

No one shall be held guilty of any penal offence on account of any act or omission which did not constitute a penal offence, under national or international law, at the time when it was committed. Nor shall a heavier penalty be imposed than the one that was applicable at the time the penal offence was committed.

Article 12
No one shall be subjected to arbitrary interference with his privacy, family, home or correspondence, nor to attacks upon his honour and reputation. Everyone has the right to the protection of the law against such interference or attacks.

Article 13
Everyone has the right to freedom of movement and residence within the borders of each State.

Everyone has the right to leave any country, including his own, and to return to his country.

Article 14
Everyone has the right to seek and to enjoy in other countries asylum from persecution.

This right may not be invoked in the case of prosecutions genuinely arising from non-political crimes or from acts contrary to the purposes and principles of the United Nations.

Article 15
Everyone has the right to a nationality.

No one shall be arbitrarily deprived of his nationality nor denied the right to change his nationality.

Article 16
Men and women of full age, without any limitation due to race, nationality or religion, have the right to marry and to found a family. They are entitled to equal rights as to marriage, during marriage and at its dissolution.

Marriage shall be entered into only with the free and full consent of the intending spouses.

The family is the natural and fundamental group unit of society and is entitled to protection by society and the State.

Article 17
Everyone has the right to own property alone as well as in association with others.

No one shall be arbitrarily deprived of his property.

Article 18
Everyone has the right to freedom of thought, conscience and religion; this right includes freedom to change his religion or belief, and freedom, either alone or in community with others and in public or private, to manifest his religion or belief in teaching, practice, worship and observance.

Article 19
Everyone has the right to freedom of opinion and expression; this right includes freedom to hold opinions without interference and to seek, receive and impart information and ideas through any media and regardless of frontiers.

Article 20
Everyone has the right to freedom of peaceful assembly and association.

No one may be compelled to belong to an association.

Article 21
Everyone has the right to take part in the government of his country, directly or through freely chosen representatives.

Everyone has the right to equal access to public service in his country.

The will of the people shall be the basis of the authority of government; this will shall be expressed in periodic and genuine elections which shall be by universal and equal suffrage and shall be held by secret vote or by equivalent free voting procedures.

Article 22
Everyone, as a member of society, has the right to social security and is entitled to realization, through national effort and international cooperation and in accordance with the organization and resources of each State, of the economic, social and cultural rights indispensable for his dignity and the free development of his personality.

Article 23
Everyone has the right to work, to free choice of employment, to just and favourable conditions of work and to protection against unemployment.

Everyone, without any discrimination, has the right to equal pay for equal work.

Everyone who works has the right to just and favourable remuneration ensuring for himself and his family an existence worthy of human dignity, and supplemented, if necessary, by other means of social protection.

Everyone has the right to form and to join trade unions for the protection of his interests.

Article 24
Everyone has the right to rest and leisure, including reasonable limitation of working hours and periodic holidays with pay.

Article 25
Everyone has the right to a standard of living adequate for the health and well-being of himself and of his family, including food, clothing, housing and medical care and necessary social services, and the right to security in the event of unemployment, sickness, disability, widowhood, old age or other lack of livelihood in circumstances beyond his control.

Motherhood and childhood are entitled to special care and assistance. All children, whether born in or out of wedlock, shall enjoy the same social protection.

Article 26
Everyone has the right to education. Education shall be free, at least in the elementary and fundamental stages. Elementary education shall be compulsory. Technical and professional education shall be made generally available and higher education shall be equally accessible to all on the basis of merit.

Education shall be directed to the full development of the human personality and to the strengthening of respect for human rights and fundamental freedoms. It shall promote understanding, tolerance and friendship among all nations, racial or religious groups, and shall further the activities of the United Nations for the maintenance of peace.

Parents have a prior right to choose the kind of education that shall be given to their children.

Article 27
Everyone has the right freely to participate in the cultural life of the community, to enjoy the arts and to share in scientific advancement and its benefits.

Everyone has the right to the protection of the moral and material interests resulting from any scientific, literary or artistic production of which he is the author.

Article 28
Everyone is entitled to a social and international order in which the rights and freedoms set forth in this Declaration can be fully realized.

Article 29
Everyone has duties to the community in which alone the free and full development of his personality is possible.

In the exercise of his rights and freedoms, everyone shall be subject only to such limitations as are determined by law solely for the purpose of securing due recognition and respect for the rights and freedoms of others and of meeting the just requirements of morality, public order and the general welfare in a democratic society.

These rights and freedoms may in no case be exercised contrary to the purposes and principles of the United Nations.

Article 30
Nothing in this Declaration may be interpreted as implying for any State, group or person any right to engage in any activity or to perform any act aimed at the destruction of any of the rights and freedoms set forth herein.

Notes

1 INTRODUCTION

1. International Covenant on Civil and Political Rights, Article 20.
2. See Human Rights Committee, 58th session, CCPR/C/58/D/550-/1993, 16 December 1996, p. 15.
3. Cf. Abdullahi Ahmed An-Na'im, *Toward an Islamic Reformation: Civil Liberties, Human Rights and International Law*, Syracuse: Syracuse University Press, 1990, pp. 182 ff.
4. See below, Chapter 3.
5. For the texts of these documents see, for instance, Walter Laqueur and Barry Rubin (eds), *The Human Rights Reader*, New York: New American Library, rev. edn, 1989, pp. 59 ff.
6. International Law Association, *Report on the Status of the Universal Declaration of Human Rights in National and International Law*, 1994, pp. 525–63.
7. See Pieter van Dijk, 'A Common Standard of Achievement: About Universal Validity and Uniform Interpretation of International Human Rights Norms', in Peter R. Baehr, Fried van Hoof, Liu Nanlai, Tao Zhenghua and Jacqueline Smith (eds), *Human Rights: Chinese and Dutch Perspectives*, The Hague/London/Boston: Martinus Nijhoff Publishers, 1996, p. 68.
8. H. Meijers and A. Nollkaemper, 'De Universele Verklaring van de Rechten van de Mens bevat thans Bindend Verdragsrecht' ['The Universal Declaration of Human Rights now contains Binding Treaty Law'], *Nederlands Juristenblad*, vol. 72 (20 June 1997), pp. 1113–15.
9. Thomas Buergenthal, *International Human Rights in a Nutshell*, St Paul, Minn.: West Publishing Co., 1988, p. 32.
10. See 'The Syracusa Principles on the Limitations and Derogation Provisions in the International Covenant on Civil and Political Rights', *Human Rights Quarterly*, vol. 7 (February 1985), pp. 3 ff.
11. K. Vasak, 'For the Third Generation of Human Rights: the Rights of Solidarity', Inaugural Lecture to the Tenth Study Session of the International Institute of Human Rights, 2–27 July 1979; Cees Flinterman, 'Three Generations of Human Rights', in Jan Berting *et al.* (eds), *Human Rights in a Pluralist World: Individuals and Collectivities*, Westport and London: Meckler, 1990, pp. 75–82.
12. Marlies Galenkamp, 'Collective Rights,' *SIM Special*, no. 16, Utrecht: SIM, 1995, pp. 53–102; Advisory Committee, on Human Rights and Foreign Policy, *Collective Rights*, Advice no. 19, The Hague: Ministry of Foreign Affairs, May 1995. Vasak, op. cit. note 12, states: 'Human rights of the third generation are those born of the obvious brotherhood of men of their indispensable solidarity; rights which would unite men in a finite world.'
13. The Soviet Union even succeeded in having the UN General Assembly adopt a resolution on the subject: UNGA Resolution 39/11 (1984).

14. Katarina Tomaševski, 'The Right to Peace', in Richard Pierre Claude and Burns H. Weston (eds), *Human Rights in the World Community: Issues and Action*, Philadelphia: University of Pennsylvania Press, 1989, p. 168 [Reprinted from: *Current Research on Peace and Violence*, vol. 5 (1982), pp. 42–69].

15. The first draft-text was introduced by the Soviet Union. See Manfred Nowak, *U.N. Covenant on Civil and Political Rights: CCPR Commentary*, Kehl/Strasbourg/Arlington: N.P. Engel Publisher, 1993, pp. 10 ff.

16. Flinterman, op. cit. p. 76, note 11.

2 UNIVERSALISM VERSUS CULTURAL RELATIVISM

1. UN General Assembly, *Official Records*, 183rd plenary meeting, 10 December 1948.

2. Cf. Antonio Cassese, *Human Rights in a Changing World*, Cambridge: Polity Press, 1990, p. 37.

3. See Philip Alston, 'The Universal Declaration at 35: Western and Passé or Alive and Universal', *The Review of the International Commission of Jurists*, No. 31 (December 1983), pp. 60–70. See also: *The Universal Declaration of Human Rights: Its Significance in 1988*, SIM Special No. 9, Utrecht: SIM, 1989; James W. Nickel, *Making Sense of Human Rights: Philosophical Reflections on the Universal Declaration of Human Rights*, Berkeley: University of California Press, 1987; Asbjørn Eide, *et al.* (eds), *The Universal Declaration of Human Rights: a Commentary*, London: Scandinavian University Press, 1992.

4. Cf. Adamantia Pollis and Peter Schwab, 'Human Rights: a Western Construct with Limited Applicability', in Pollis and Schwab (eds), *Human Rights: Ideological and Cultural Perspectives*, New York: Praeger, 1980, p. 14. See also C. Tomuschat, 'Is Universality of Human Rights Standards an Outdated and Utopian Concept?' in E. Bieber (ed.), *Das Europa der Zweiten Generation* ['The Europe of the Second Generation'], Munich: Engel Verlag, 1981. The prime minister of Malaysia, Mahathir bin Mohamad, has asked for a revision of the Universal Declaration, which 'was formulated by the superpowers, which did not understand the need of poor countries' (*International Herald Tribune*, 29 July 1997). See also Dato' Param Cumaraswamy, 'The Universal Declaration of Human Rights: Is It Universal?' *Human Rights Solidarity*, vol. 7 (December 1997), pp. 23–5.

5. See R. Panikkar, 'Is the Notion of Human Rights a Western Concept?' *Diogenes* 120 (1985), p. 75.

6. United Nations General Assembly, A/CONF.157/23, 12 July 1993, *Vienna Declaration and Programme of Action*, par. 5.

7. Ibid.

8. See G.J.H. van Hoof, 'Asian Challenges to the Concept of Universality: Afterthoughts on the Vienna Conference on Human Rights', in Peter R. Baehr, Fried van Hoof, Liu Nanlai, Tao Zhenghua and Jacqueline Smith (eds), *Human Rights: Chinese and Dutch Perspectives*, The Hague/London/Boston: Martinus Nijhoff Publishers, 1996, pp. 1–15.

9. *Our Voice: Bangkok NGO Declaration on Human Rights*, Bangkok: Asian Cultural Forum on Development, 1993, p. 199.

10. See, for an excellent survey of relevant views, Alison Dundes Renteln, *International Human Rights: Universalism versus Relativism*, Newbury Park: Sage, 1990. For a defence of cultural relativism, see Pollis/ Schwab, op. cit. (note 4), pp. 1–18; also Adamantia Pollis, 'Towards a New Universalism: Reconstruction and Dialogue', *Netherlands Quarterly of Human Rights*, vol. 16 (March 1998), pp. 5–23. For a strong rejection of cultural relativism: Rhoda E. Howard, 'Cultural Absolutism and the Nostalgia for Community', *Human Rights Quarterly*, vol. 15 (May 1993), pp. 315–38.

11. Peter R. Baehr, 'Amnesty International and its Self-Imposed Limited Mandate', *Netherlands Quarterly of Human Rights*, vol. 12 (1994), pp. 18–19.

12. Since then, Amnesty has acted in many countries on matters regarding the violation of human rights of homosexuals. Amnesty International, *Violations of the Human Rights of Homosexuals*, AI Index: POL 30/01/94, January 1994. In May 1996, the Dutch section of Amnesty International, in cooperation with a number of other groups, organized a public manifestation on the theme 'Homosexuality and Human Rights'. See: Amnesty International, *OUTfront! Human Rights and Sexual Identity*, *http://amnestyusa.org/OUTfront*.

13. Jack Donnelly, *Universal Human Rights in Theory and Practice*, Ithaca and London: Cornell University Press, 1989, p. 57.

14. Statement by Mr Ali Alatas, Foreign Minister of Indonesia, before the Second World Conference on Human Rights, Vienna, 14 June 1993.

15. See Economic and Social Council, *Draft Optional Protocol Providing for the Consideration of Communications. Report Submitted by Mr. Philip Alston*, E/C.12/1994/12, 9 November 1994. In January 1995, the Netherlands Institute of Human Rights (SIM) convened an international meeting of experts which discussed this idea and prepared the text for a draft Optional Protocol. See Fons Coomans and Fried van Hoof (eds), *The Right to complain about Economic, Social and Cultural Rights*, SIM Special No. 18, Utrecht: SIM, 1995; Kitty Arambulo, *Strengthening the Supervision of the International Covenant on Economic Social and Cultural Rights*, Antwerp/Groningen/Oxford: Intersentia/Hart, 1999.

16. Cf. Julian Burger and Paul Hunt, 'Towards the International Protection of Indigenous Peoples' Rights', *Netherlands Quarterly of Human Rights*, vol. 12 (1994), pp. 405–23; Draft Declaration on the Rights of Indigenous Peoples, E/C.4/Sub.2/1993/29, pp. 50–60, reprinted in *Netherlands Quarterly of Human Rights*, vol. 12 (1994), pp. 471–9. See also (Netherlands) Advisory Committee on Human Rights and Foreign Policy, *Indigenous Peoples, Advisory Report* no. 16, The Hague, 8 June 1993 and the reaction by the Ministers of Foreign Affairs and for Development Cooperation.

17. Vienna Declaration and Programme of Action, op. cit. (note 6), par. I.1.

18. Ibid., par. I.4.

19. Statement by Alatas, op. cit. (note 14).

20. Pieter van Dijk, 'A Common Standard of Achievement: about Universal Validity and Uniform Interpretation of International Human Rights

Norms', in Baehr/VanHoof/Liu Nanlai/Tao Zhenghua/Smith (eds), op. cit. (note 8), p. 75.
21. Bangladesh, Brunei Darussalam, China, Indonesia, Kuwait, Lao People's Democratic Republic, Malaysia, the Maldives, Myanmar, Oman, Pakistan, Thailand and the United Arab Emirates. (Six other Asian states that have not ratified the covenants did not participate in the Bangkok Conference: Kazakhstan, Kyrgyzstan, Saudi Arabia, Tajikistan, Turkmenistan and Uzbekistan.) China has called attention to the fact that it has acceded to eight (other) international conventions on human rights. (See speech by Mr Liu Huaqiu, head of the Chinese delegation at the World Conference on Human Rights, Vienna, 15 June 1993.) In the fall of 1997, China signed the International Covenant on Economic, Social and Cultural Rights which it ratified in 2001. It has also signed (but not yet ratified) the International Covenant on Civil and Political Rights.
22. Statement by Foreign Minister Wong Kan Seng of Singapore to the World Conference on Human Rights, Vienna, 16 June 1993.
23. Though it should be stressed that in Asia the notion of cultural relativism is adhered to by governments of states that are by no means among the poorest, such as China, Malaysia and Singapore.
24. The text of the draft declaration has been reprinted in *Netherlands Quarterly of Human Rights*, vol. 15 (December 1997), pp. 546–50. Among the signers of the Declaration were former German Chancellor Helmut Schmidt, former US President Jimmy Carter, former Soviet President Mikhail Gorbachev, former French President Valéry Giscard d'Estaing and some 20 other former government leaders. For a critical comment, see Fried van Hoof, 'A Universal Declaration of Human Responsibilities: Far-Sighted or Flawed?' in Mielle Bulterman, Aart Hendriks, Jacqueline Smith, *To Baehr in Our Minds: Essays on Human Rights from the Heart of the Netherlands*, SIM Special No. 21, Utrecht: SIM, 1998, pp. 55–69.
25. Theo van Boven, 'A Universal Declaration of Human Responsibilities?' in Barend van der Heijden and Bahia Tahrib Lie (eds), *Reflections on the Universal Dedaration of Human Rights*, The Hague/London/Boston: Martinus Nijhoff Publishers, 1998, pp. 73–9.
26. R.J. Vincent, *Human Rights and International Relations*, Cambridge: Cambridge University Press, 1986, p. 105.
27. Antonio Cassese, *Human Rights in a Changing World*, Cambridge: Polity Press, 1990, p. 66.
28. See Chapter 10.
29. Op. cit. (note 9), p. 243.

3   GROSS AND SYSTEMATIC VIOLATIONS

1. Cecilia Medina Quiroga, *The Battle of Human Rights: Gross, Systematic Violations and the Inter-American System*, Dordrecht/Boston/London: Martinus Nijhoff Publishers, 1988, p. 16.
2. The latter term has become familiar since the conflict in the former Yugoslavia.

3. 'Annan Says Hundreds of Thousands Live as Slaves', *UN Around the World*, 3 December 1997.
4. *Prisma van de Mensenrechten* ['Prism of Human Rights'], Amsterdam: Amnesty International, 1992, p. 178.
5. See A.H. Robertson and J.G. Merrils, *Human Rights in the World: an Introduction to the Study of the International Protection of Human Rights*, Manchester and New York: Manchester University Press, 4th edn, 1996, pp. 15–17.
6. International Covenant on Civil and Political Rights, Art. 8; European Convention on Human Rights and Fundamental Freedoms, Art. 4; American Convention on Human Rights, Art. 6; African Charter on Human Rights and Peoples' Rights, Art. 5.
7. See Report of the Working Group on Contemporary Forms of Slavery on its twenty-second session (11 July 1997), E/CN.4/Sub.2/1997/13.
8. Asbjørn Eide, 'The Sub-Commission on Prevention of Discrimination and Protection of Minorities', in Philip Alston (ed.), *The United Nations and Human Rights*, Oxford: Clarendon Press, 1992, p. 235.
9. See Marieke Klap, Yvonne Klerk, Jacqueline Smith (eds), *Combatting Traffic in Persons*, SIM Special No. 17, Utrecht: SIM, 1995.
10. Universal Declaration of Human Rights, Art. 3; Convention on the Prevention and Punishment of the Crime of Genocide, Art. 2; International Covenant on Civil and Political Rights, Art. 6; European Convention on Human Rights and Fundamental Freedoms, Art. 2; American Convention on Human Rights, Art. 4; African Charter on Human Rights and Peoples' Rights, Art. 4.
11. See, for example, Sarah Joseph, 'Denouement of the Deaths on the Rock: the Right to Life of Terrorists', *Netherlands Quarterly of Human Rights*, vol. 14 (March 1996), pp. 5–22. The article discusses the McCann judgement of the European Court of Human Rights, which stated that the shooting of three unarmed members of the Irish Republic Army in Gibraltar by British security agents constitued a violation of Article 2 of the European Convention (the right to life).
12. Article 6 of the International Covenant on Civil and Political Rights was drafted with the intention of indicating that the death penalty should be abolished. See Robertson/Merrils, op. cit. (note 5), p. 37.
13. Including Amnesty International as well as the present author.
14. See Eric Prokosch, 'The Cruelty of the Death Penalty: Capital Punishment and Human Rights', Parliamentary Assembly of the Council of Europe, Seminar on the Abolition of the Death Penalty, Kiev (Ukraine), 28–29 November 1996, AS/Jur (1996), p. 72. See also Amnesty International, *When the State Kills...: the Death Penalty v. Human Rights*, London, 1989, p. 5: 'Whatever purpose is cited, the idea that a government can justify a punishment as cruel as death conflicts with the very concept of human rights. The significance of human rights is precisely that some means may *never* be used to protect society because their use violates the very values which may make society worth protecting' [italics supplied].
15. Amnesty International, *Abolitionist and Retentionist Countries*, www.web.amnesty.org/ last updated 23 November 2000.

16. Amnesty International, *Death Sentences and Executions in 2000*, www.web.amnesty.org. Eighty-eight per cent of all known executions took place in China (1000), Saudi Arabia (123), the United States (85) and Iran (75).
17. Of the 50 US states, 38 now provide for the death penalty in law. Over 3600 prisoners were under sentence of death as of 1 September 1999. Amnesty International, *Facts and Figures on the Death Penalty*, www.web.amnesty.org/ last updated 16 November 2000.
18. Only the American Convention on Human Rights states explicitly, in Article 4: 'Every person has the right to have his life respected. This right shall be protected by law, and, in general, *from the moment of conception*' [italics supplied].
19. Oregon is the only state of the United States where euthanasia by request is permitted, under stringent conditions. See further, Constantijn Kelk, 'Towards the Decriminalisation of Euthanasia in the Netherlands?' in Mielle Bulterman, Aart Hendriks, Jacqueline Smith (eds), *To Baehr in Our Minds: Essays on Human Rights from the Heart of the Netherlands*, SIM Special No. 21, Utrecht: SIM, 1998, pp. 349–67.
20. Universal Declaration of Human Rights, Art. 5; International Covenant on Civil and Political Rights, Art. 7; European Convention on Human Rights and Fundamental Freedoms, Art. 3; American Convention on Human Rights, Art. 5 (2); African Charter on Human Rights and Peoples' Rights, Art. 6; International Convention against Torture and Other Cruel, Inhuman or Degrading Treatment of Punishment. See also Pieter H. Kooijmans, 'Opening Address: Torturers and their Masters', in: Roland D. Crelinsten and Alex P. Schmid (eds), *The Politics of Pain: Torturers and their Masters*, Leiden: COMT, 1993, pp. 16–17: 'In only two cases in my six years' experience as Special Rapporteur have I received a reply from a government in which it was stated that under the particular circumstances the alleged treatment was justified or that it did not constitute torture.'
21. International Convention against Torture and Other Cruel, Inhuman, or Degrading Treatment or Punishment, Art. 1. The concept of 'cruel, inhuman or degrading treatment or punishment' is not defined in the Treaty. Kooijmans has made the point that torture is a stronger form of cruel or inhuman treatment: 'There is no real difference and the question where torture ends and cruel treatment begins, is so subjective that one cannot work with it' (P.H. Kooijmans, 'Foltering – een Onuitroeibaar Kwaad?' ['Torture – an Evil that Cannot be Eradicated?'] *Ars Aequi*, vol. 42 (January 1993), p. 39; my translation from the original Dutch).
22. Kooijmans, op. cit. (note 21), p. 39.
23. Kooijmans, op. cit. (note 21), p. 40.
24. Herbert C. Kelman, 'The Social Context of Torture: Policy Process and Authority Structure', in Crelinsten and Schmid, op. cit. (note 20), p. 23.
25. Ronald D. Crelinsten, 'In their Own Words: the World of the Torturer', in Crelinsten and Schmid, op. cit. (note 20), pp. 53 ff. Kelman refers to the involvement of the United States in training torturers in Central America, op. cit. (note 24), p. 28.
26. Crelinsten quotes from an interrogator's manual of the Khmer Rouge: 'The purpose of torturing is to get their responses. It's not something we do

for the fun of it. Thus we must make them hurt so that they will respond quickly' (Roland D. Crelinsten, 'In their Own Words: the World of the Torturer', in: Crelinsten and Schmid, op. cit. (note 20), p. 39; see also p. 42).

27.   When this issue was debated at the Dutch Naval Academy, an experienced naval officer remarked that in such a situation he would apply the prohibited act of torture *himself*. He did not consider it acceptable to give such an order to a subordinate.

28.   Kelman, op. cit. (note 24), p. 31 refers to the protection of the state against internal and external threats to state security as a fundamental objective and justification of torture.

29.   See Amnesty International, 'The Draft Optional Protocol to the Convention against Torture', AI INDEX: IOR 51/01/96 (July 1996).

30.   Raphael Lemkin, *Axis Rule in Occupied Europe*, Washington DC: Carnegie Endowment for International Peace, 1944. For a review of Lemkin's work, see Lawrence J. LeBlanc, *The United States and the Genocide Convention*, Durham and London: Duke University Press, 1991, pp. 17–22.

31.   Cf. the extensive literature on the Holocaust; among others: Raul Hilberg, *The Destruction of the European Jews*, New York: New Viewpoints, 1973; Lucy Dawidowicz, *The War against the Jews, 1933–1945*, New York: Holt, Rinehart and Winston, 1975; Gerald Fleming, *Hitler and the Final Solution*, Berkeley: University of California Press, 1985; Israel Gutman (ed.), *Encyclopedia of the Holocaust*, New York: Macmillan, 1990, and Daniel Jonah Goldhagen, *Hitler's Willing Executioners: Ordinary Germans and the Holocaust*, London: Abacus, 1997.

32.   See Richard G. Hovanissian, 'Ethiology and Sequelae of the Armenian Genocide', in George J. Andreopoulos (ed.), *Genocide: Conceptual and Historical Dimensions*, Philadelphia: University of Pennsylvania Press, 1997, pp. 111–40.

33.   See the following contributions in the volume edited by Andreopoulos, op. cit. (note 32): Leo Kuper, 'Theoretical Issues Relating to Genocide: Uses and Abuses', (pp. 31–46); Frank Chalk, 'Redefining Genocide' (pp. 47–63); Israel W. Charny, 'Toward a Generic Definition of Genocide' (pp. 64–94), and Helen Fein, 'Genocide, Terror, Life Integrity, and War Crimes: the Case for Discrimination' (pp. 95–107).

34.   Martin van Bruinessen, 'Genocide in Kurdistan? The Suppression of the Dersim Rebellion in Turkey (1937–38) and the Chemical War against the Iraqi Kurds (1988)', in Andreopoulos, op. cit. (note 32), p. 156: 'I am reluctant to use the term genocide for the Iraqi regime's chemical warfare against the Kurds, although it has been argued that this case appears to fit the definition of the 1948 Convention. The final verdict will probably hinge on the question of intent.'

35.   UN Sub-Commission for the Prevention of Discrimination and the Protection of Minorities, *Convention on the Prevention and Punishment of the Crime of Genocide*, E/CN.4/Sub.2/1993/6, 16.

36.   See Ben Kieman, 'The Cambodian Genocide: Issues and Responses', in Andreopoulos, op. cit. (note 32), pp. 191–4; Roel A. Burgler, 'The Case of Cambodia: the Khmer Rouge's Reign of Terror', in Albert J. Jongman (ed.), *Contemporary Genocides: Causes, Cases, Consequences*, Leiden: PIOOM, 1996, pp. 59–76.

37. See Sophyke de Voogd, 'Het Genocideverdrag: een Dode Letter?' ['The Genocide Convention: a Dead Letter?'], *Transaktie*, vol. 24 (December 1995), p. 485.

38. 'Considered in the context of the conflicts in the former Yugoslavia, "ethnic cleansing" means rendering an area ethnically homogeneous by using force or intimidation to remove persons or given groups from the area.' (*Final Report of the Commission of Experts Established Pursuant to Security Council Resolution 780 (1992)*, UN SCOR, Annex 1, para. 129, UN Doc. S/1994/674 (1994), as cited in Todd A. Salzman, 'Rape Camps as a Means of Ethnic Cleansing: Religious, Cultural, and Ethical Responses to Rape Victims in the Former Yugoslavia', *Human Rights Quarterly*, vol. 20 (May 1998), p. 354).

39. UN Security Council, *Report of the Secretary-General Pursuant to Paragraph 2 of Security Council Resolution 808 (1993)*, S/25704, 3 May 1993, p. 4.

40. David Rohde, *A Safe Area: Srebrenica – Europe's Worst Massacre since the Second World War*, London: Pocket Books, 1997. See also Jan Willem Honig and Norbert Both, *Srebrenica: Record of a War Crime*, Harmondsworth: Penguin, 1996.

41. The United States government has taken the position that the Serbian role in Bosnia 'border[ed] on genocide' and that certain activities were 'tantamount to genocide' or represented 'acts of genocide'. See 'Is it Genocide or Isn't It?', *International Herald Tribune*, 15 February 1994. UN Secretary-General Boutros Ghali had no doubt that in Rwanda genocide had been committed (see Boutros Boutros-Ghali, 'Genocide: When Will We Ever Learn?' *International Herald Tribune*, 6 April 1995). This view was shared by Amnesty International, which explicitly included the Rwandan situation in its considerations; see Amnesty International, 'Rwanda and Burundi: Horror of Genocide Hangs over the Region One Year Later', AI INDEX: AFR 47/WU 03/95, 6 April 1995.

42. For the text of the Statute, see *Netherlands Quarterly of Human Rights*, vol. 11 (1993), pp. 503–12.

43. For the Statute of the Rwanda Tribunal, see UN Security Council resolution 955 (1994), S/RES/955, adopted 8 November 1994. In paragraph 1 of this resolution the Tribunal is established 'for the sole purpose of prosecuting persons responsible for genocide and other serious violations of international humanitarian law committed in the territory of Rwanda'.

44. 'Panel Opens Genocide Case against Serb Leaders', *International Herald Tribune*, 28 June 1996.

45. See De Voogd, op. cit. (note 37), pp. 483–4. See also Albert J. Jongman, 'Contemporary Genocides: the Need for More Effective Prevention', in Jongman, op. cit. (note 36), pp. 1–16.

46. For a thorough treatment of the subject, see Reed Brody, Felipe Gonzáles, 'Nunca Más: an Analysis of International Instruments on "Disappearances"', *Human Rights Quarterly*, vol. 19 (May 1997), pp. 365–405.

47. Amnesty International consistently puts the term in quotation marks to indicate that the person in question has not really 'disappeared', but has probably been abducted by the security forces.

48. In later years the phenomenon has spread to countries outside Latin America, e.g. Uganda, the Philippines, Sri Lanka and, more recently, Turkey and the former Yugoslavia.
49. See Iain Guest, *Behind the Disappearances: Argentina's Dirty War against Human Rights and the United Nations*, Philadelphia: University of Pennsylvania Press, 1990, pp. 49 ff.
50. UN General Assembly Resolution 47/33, 18 December 1992.
51. Ibid., Article 1, paragraph 2.
52. OAS Doc. OEA/Ser.P/AG/Doc.3114/94.
53. Ibid. Article II.
54. Velásquez-Rodriguez case, No. 7920 (29 July 1988).
55. Philip Alston, 'The Commission on Human Rights', in Alston, op. cit. (note 8), p. 177.
56. Amnesty International USA, *'Disappearances': a Workbook*, New York, 1981, p. 126.
57. Working Group on Enforced or Involuntary Disappearances, Press Release, 61st session, 21–25 August 2000.
58. Ibid.
59. *Report of the Working Group on Enforced or Involuntary Disappearances* E/CN.4/2001/68, 18 December 2000.
60. Op. cit. (note 52). For the origin of both instruments, see Brody/ Gonzáles, op. cit. (note 46), pp. 371–5.
61. See Brody/Gonzáles, op. cit. (note 46), pp. 378–82.
62. Ibid., pp. 382–3.
63. Amnesty International, '"Destination Unknown": "Disappeared" in Former Yugoslavia: Recommendations', AI INDEX: EUR 05/06/95 (October 1995) and '"An Unknown Destination": "Disappeared" in Former Yugoslavia. Case Sheets', AI INDEX: EUR 05/08/95, October 1995.
64. See Chapter 9.

4 ECONOMIC AND SOCIAL RIGHTS

1. See, for cultural rights, Rodolfo Stavenhagen, 'Cultural Rights and Universal Human Rights' and Asbjørn Eide, 'Cultural Rights as Individual Human Rights', in Asbjørn Eide, Catarina Krause, Allan Rosas (eds), *Economic, Social and Cultural Rights: a Textbook*, Dordrecht/Boston/ London: Martinus Nijhoff Publishers, 1995, pp. 63–77 and 229–40. The present chapter deals mainly with economic and social rights.
2. Vienna Declaration and Programme of Action, adopted by the World Conference on Human Rights on 25 June 1993, UN Doc. A/Conf.157/23, Part I, par. 5.
3. 'The third is freedom from want – which translated into world terms, means economic understandings, which will secure to every nation a healthy peace time life for its inhabitants – everywhere in the world.' By way of comment, he later added (in his State of the Union speech of January 1944): 'We have come to the clear realization of the fact that true individual freedom cannot exist without economic security and independence. "Necessitous men are not free men." People who are hungry and out of a job are the stuff of which dictatorships are made' (cited in Asbjørn Eide,

'Economic, Social and Cultural Rights as Human Rights', in Eide/Krause/ Rosas, op. cit. (note 1), 29). The other three freedoms he mentioned were freedom of expression, freedom of religion, and freedom from fear, especially the threat of war (see Samuel I Rosenmann (ed.), *The Public Papers of F.D. Roosevelt*, New York: Russell & Russell, 1969, vol. 9, 663).

4. See Philip Alston, 'U.S. Ratification of the Covenant on Economic, Social and Cultural Rights: the Need for an Entirely New Strategy', *American Journal of International Law*, vol. 84 (1990), pp. 365–92. It is for this reason that the United States has never ratified the International Covenant on Economic, Social and Cultural Rights.

5. 'In most ministries [in the Netherlands], the view seems to persist that the ICESCR [International Covenant on Economic, Social and Cultural Rights] is still but a "poor relation" of its sibling Covenant, the International Covenant on Civil and Political Rights' (Netherlands Lawyers' Committee for Human Rights, Commentary on the Second Periodic report of the Netherlands submitted in accordance with Art. 16 of the ICESCR, 8 December 1997, p. 4).

6. See A.P.M. Coomans, 'Schendingen van Economische, Sociale en Culturele Rechten' ['Violations of Economic, Social and Cultural Rights'], in A.P.M. Coomans, A.W. Heringa, I. Westendorp (eds), *De Toenemende Betekenis van Economische, Sociale en Culturele Rechten* ['The Increasing Significance of Economic, Social and Cultural Rights'], Leiden: Stichting NJCM-Boekerij, 1994, p. 59.

7. UN Doc. E/CN.4/Sub.2/1987/23.

8. See Coomans, op. cit. (note 6), p. 72. Van Hoof has mentioned a fourth obligation: 'the obligation to promote', see: G.J.H. van Hoof, 'The Legal Nature of Economic, Social and Cultural Rights', in P. Alston and K. Tomaševski (eds), *The Right to Food*, Utrecht: Studie en Informatiecentrum Mensenrechten, 1984, pp. 106–7. Eide has later also added another obligation to his typology: 'the obligation to assist'; see Eide/ Krause/Rosas, op. cit. (note 1), pp. 169–88.

9. See Krysztof Drzewicki, 'The Right to Work and Rights in Work', in Eide/Krause/Rosas, op. cit. (note 1), pp. 169–88.

10. See Martin Scheinin, 'The Right to Social Security', in Eide/Krause/ Rosas, op. cit. (note 1), pp. 159–67.

11. See Asbjørn Eide, 'The Right to an Adequate Standard of Living Including the Right to Food', in Eide/Krause/Rosas, op. cit. (note 1), pp. 89–105; Katarina Tomaševski, 'Defining Violations of the Right to Food', in Coomans/Van Hoof (eds), in cooperation with Kitty Arambulo, Jacqueline Smith, Brigit Toebes, *The Right to Complain about Economic, Social and Cultural Rights*, SIM Special No. 18, Utrecht: SIM, 1995, pp. 115–25, with comments by Rolf Künneman, pp. 127–41.

12. See Scott Leckie, 'The Right to Housing', in Eide/Krause/Rosas, op. cit. (note 1), pp. 107–23; Scott Leckie, 'The Justiciability of Housing Rights', in Coomans/Van Hoof, op. cit. (note 11), pp. 35–76, with comment by David Harris, pp. 103–8.

13. See Katarina Tomaševski, 'Health Rights', in Eide/Krause/Rosas, op. cit. (note 1), pp. 125–42; Virginia Leary, 'The Right to Complain: the Right to Health', in Coomans/Van Hoof, op. cit. (note 11), pp. 12–26 and

comment by Bruno Simma, pp. 27–31. See also Brigit Toebes, *The Right to Health as a Human Right in International Law*, Antwerp/Groningen/ Oxford: Intersentia/Hart, 1999.

14. See Manfred Nowak, 'The Right to Education', in Eide/Krause/Rosas, op. cit. (note 1), pp. 189–211; Fons Coomans, 'Clarifying the Core Elements of the Right to Education', in Coomans/Van Hoof, op. cit. (note 11), pp. 12–26 and comment by Bruno Simma, pp. 27–31.

15. See Katarina Tomaševski, 'Environmental Rights', in Eide/Krause/ Rosas, op. cit. (note 1), pp. 257–69.

16. See Subrata Roy Chowdhury, Erik M.G. Denters, Paul J.I.M. de Waart (eds), *The Right to Development in International Law*, Dordrecht/Boston/ London: Martinus Nijhoff Publishers, 1992.

17. For collective rights, see further Chapter 5.

18. See, for example, Asbjørn Eide, 'Economic, Social and Cultural Rights as Human Rights', in Eide/Krause/Rosas, op. cit. (note 1), pp. 21–40.

19. See B.G. Ramcharan, 'Implementation of the International Covenant on Economic, Social and Cultural Rights', *Netherlands International Law Review*, vol. 23 (1976), pp. 151–61.

20. See *Official Records of the Economic and Social Council*, 1989, Supplement No. 4 (E/1989/22), Annex III.

21. The Raoul Wallenberg Institute in Lund (Sweden) has compiled the first seven comments in a handy publication: *General Comments or Recommendations Adopted by the United Nations Human Rights Treaty Bodies, volume II: Committee on Economic, Social and Cultural Rights*, Lund, 1997. The first volume contains the general comments by the UN Human Rights Committee regarding the International Covenant on Civil and Political Rights.

22. 'Limburg Principles on the Implementation of the International Covenant on Economic, Social and Cultural Rights', *Human Rights Quarterly*, vol. 9 (1987), pp. 122–35; also in UN Doc. E/CN.4/1987/17, 8 January 1987.

23. See B.A. Andreassen, T. Skålnes, A.G. Smith and H. Stokke, 'Assessing Human Rights Performance in Developing Countries: the Case for a Minimum Threshold Approach', in B.A. Andreassen, A. Eide (eds), *Human Rights in Developing Countries 1987/1988*, Kopenhagen: Akademisk Forlag 1988, pp. 333–56.

24. Coomans, op. cit. (note 6), p. 61.

25. See Eide, op. cit. (note 1), p. 29 about the preparation of the Universal Declaration of Human Rights during the war years: 'The realization, particularly in the West, that the political upheavals and the emergence of totalitarian regimes in the period between the two World Wars had been due to the widespread unemployment and poverty, led to a genuine interest in securing economic and social rights, not only for their own sake but also for the preservation of individual freedom and democracy. This view was based on a conviction that *even in periods of recession* it would be necessary to ensure that basic economic and social rights should be enjoyed by all' [italics supplied].

26. See, for violations of economic, social and cultural rights, Theo C. van Boven, Cees Flinterman, Ingrid Westendorp (eds), *The Maastricht*

Guidelines on Violations of Economic, Social and Cultural Rights, SIM Special No. 20, Utrecht: SIM, 1998.
27. UN Doc. E/1991/23, p. 64 and UN Doc. E/1992/23, p. 32.
28. See Milton Kothari, 'Israel and Palestine: Monitoring E.S.C. Rights', *Human Rights Tribune*, vol. 4 (1997), pp. 14–15.
29. Amnesty International, *Report 2001*.
30. See Katarina Tomaševski, 'Women', in Eide/Krause/Rosas, op. cit. (note 1), pp. 273–88.
31. Zwaan-De Vries vs the Netherlands, comm. No. 182/1984 and Broeks vs the Netherlands, comm. No. 172/1984.
32. As quoted in Martin Scheinin, 'Economic and Social Rights as Legal Rights', in Eide/Krause/Rosas, op. cit. (note 1), p. 44.
33. UN Doc. E/C.12/1992/WP.9.
34. UN Doc. A/CONF.157/23, op. cit. (note 2), p. 25, par. 75.
35. UN Doc. E/C.12/1994/12 (9 November 1994). A recent Committee draft is to be found in document E/CN.4/1997/105 (18 December 1996).
36. Coomans/Van Hoof, op. cit. (note 11).
37. See Martin Scheinin, 'Economic and Social Rights as Legal Rights', in Eide/Krause/Rosas, op. cit. (note 1), pp. 41–62.
38. Scott Leckie, 'The Justiciability of Housing Rights', in Coomans/Van Hoof, op. cit. (note 11), p. 37.
39. 'NJCM Commentary on the Draft Optional Protocol to the International Covenant on Economic, Social and Cultural Rights', 1 December 1997, not published.
40. Advisory Committee on Human Rights and Foreign Policy, *Economic, Social and Cultural Human Rights*, Advisory Report No. 18, The Hague: Ministry of Foreign Affairs, 1994, pp. 15–16 (official English version).
41. There is also the Asian Coalition for Housing Rights and Habitat International Coalition; see Scott Leckie, 'The Legal Struggle for Housing Rights: One NGO's Search for the Elusive', *Beyond Law*, vol. 2 (1992), pp. 75–87.
42. See Asbjørn Eide and Allan Rosas, 'Economic, Social and Cultural Rights: a Universal Challenge', in Eide/Krause/Rosas, op. cit. (note 1), p. 18: 'Most international NGOs have neglected the issue.'
43. See Chapter 10.
44. See Philip Alston, 'The Committee on Economic, Social and Cultural Rights', in Philip Alston (ed.), *The United Nations and Human Rights*, Oxford: Clarendon Press, 1992, p. 502: 'There is no doubt that the NGO community should consider itself culpable on this score. Its neglect of the only body seeking to do serious and sustained work in the field of economic, social and cultural rights tends to undermine the purported attachment by so many of its members to those rights.'
45. Katarina Tomaševski has called attention to the gap between human rights organizations and NGOs that deal with development questions. See Katarina Tomaševski, 'Indicators', in Eide/Krause/Rosas, op. cit. (note 1), p. 398. See further, Kitty Arambulo, 'Drafting an Optional Protocol to the International Covenant on Economic, Social and Cultural Rights: Can an Ideal Become Reality?' *Journal of International Law & Policy*, vol. 2 (Winter 1996), pp. 111–36.

46. 'The Forgotten Prisoners', *The Observer*, 28 May 1961.
47. Approximately 1.3 billion people live on less than $US 1 a day each; almost one billion people are illiterate; more than one billion people have no access to safe drinking water; 840 million people suffer from starvation or are facing famine; one-third of the people in developing countries do not grow older than 40 years (see UNDP, *Human Development Report 1997*, New York/Oxford: Oxford University Press, 1997). See also Asbjørn Eide, 'Obstacles and Goals to be Pursued', in Eide/Krause/Rosas, op. cit. (note 1), p. 381.
48. Twice a year, each meeting lasting three weeks, according to ECOSOC resolution 1995/39.

5 COLLECTIVE RIGHTS: THE RIGHT OF SELF-DETERMINATION

1. The African Charter on Human and Peoples' Rights contains the following collective rights: the right to existence and self-determination (Article 20), the right to natural resources (Article 21), the right to development (Article 22), the right to international peace and security (Article 23), and the right to a general satisfactory environment (Article 24).
2. Next to collective rights, terms that are used are 'solidarity rights' or 'rights of the third generation'(see Chapter 2).
3. See, for example, Philip Alston, 'A Third Generation of Solidarity Rights: Progressive Development or Obfuscation of International Human Rights Law?' *Netherlands International Law Review*, vol. 29 (1982), pp. 307–22; P.H. Kooijmans, 'Human Rights Universal Panacea? Some Reflections on the so-called Human Rights of the Third Generation', *Netherlands International Law Review*, vol. 37 (1990), pp. 315–29; Jan Berting *et al.* (eds), *Human Rights in a Pluralist World: Individuals and Collectivities*, Westport/London: Meckler, 1990; Marlies Galenkamp, *Individualism versus Collectivism: the Concept of Collective Rights*, Rotterdam: RFS, 1993; Marlies Galenkamp, 'Collective Rights', SIM Special No. 16, Utrecht: SIM, 1995, pp. 53–102.
4. Advisory Committee on Human Rights and Foreign Policy, *Collective Rights*, Advisory Report No. 19, The Hague: Ministry of Foreign Affairs, 1995, p. 35 (official English version).
5. Ibid., p. 23.
6. Cf. W.J.M. van Genugten, *Mensenrechten in Ontwikkeling: Het "Goede Doel" Voorbij* ['Human Rights in Development: Beyond the "Good Purpose"'], Nijmegen: Katholieke Universiteit, 1992, p. 27.
7. 'After extensive discussions, the Advisory Committee has failed to reach a consensus on the question of whether collective rights can be termed human rights.' (Advisory Committee on Human Rights and Foreign Policy, *Collective Rights*, op. cit. (note 4), p. 4).
8. Van Genugten, op. cit. (note 6), pp. 24 and 29.

9. Cf. Advisory Committee on Human Rights and Foreign Policy, *Collective Rights*, op. cit. (note 4), p. 5.
10. Prevailing opinion in China is quite different on this point. See Li Buyun, 'On Individual and Collective Human Rights', in Peter R. Baehr, Fried van Hoof, Liu Nanlai, Tao Zhenghua, Jacqueline Smith (eds), *Human Rights: Chinese and Dutch Perspectives*, The Hague/London/Boston: Martinus Nijhoff Publishers, 1996, p. 121: 'The subject of collective human rights consists mainly of nations, societies, countries, and groups of countries. Among them, the State is the essential subject of human rights, for today the basic unit in the international community is the State.'
11. France has made an explicit reservation with regard to Article 27 of the International Covenant on Civil and Political Rights, referring to Article 2 of the French Constitution which determines the equality under the law of all French citizens, without distinction as to origin, race or religion. The British human rights expert Nigel Rodley rightly wonders why France has found it necessary to make this reservation. Other countries whose constitutions contain a similar guarantee, have not found it necessary to enter such a reservation regarding Article 27. See Nigel Rodley, 'Conceptual Problems in the Protection of Minorities: International Legal Developments', *Human Rights Quarterly*, vol. 17 (February 1995), pp. 51–2.
12. See Manfred Nowak, *U.N. Covenant on Civil and Political Rights: CCPR Commentary*, Kehl/Strasbourg/Arlington: N.P. Engel Publishers, 1993, p. 13.
13. See Bruno Simma (ed.), *The Charter of the United Nations: a Commentary*, Oxford: Oxford University Press, p. 924: 'The point is that numerous delegates [to the founding conference of the United Nations in San Francisco] understood self-determination merely in the sense of self-government, which they in turn took to mean internal autonomy, and in some cases also a democratic constitutional system; they did not, however, connect it with any right to independent statehood.' Rosalyn Higgins has made the point that the use of the term in the Charter only referred to the protection of states against intervention by other states or governments. She has called the idea that self-determination in the Charter was meant in the present meaning of the word 'a retrospective rewriting of history' (Rosalyn Higgins, *Problems and Process: International Law and How We Use It*, Oxford: Clarendon Press, 1994, p. 111).
14. McCorquodale quotes from Harold Nicholson's diary about the way in which during the Paris Peace Conference populations were shifted around: Robert McCorquodale, 'Self-Determination: a Human Rights Approach', *International and Comparative Law Quarterly*, vol. 43 (October 1994), p. 870.
15. See Johan Willem Friso Wielenga, *West-Duitsland: Partner uit Noodzaak, Nederland en de Bondsrepubliek 1949–1955* ['West Germany: Partner out of Necessity, the Netherlands and the German Federal Republic 1949–1955'], Utrecht: Het Spectrum, 1989, p. 388. Dutch Foreign Minister Van Kleffens had originally wanted to increase the Netherlands' territory by one-third (10 000 square kilometres with one-and-a-half million German inhabitants). After the First World War, the German territory of Eupen

and Malmédy was joined with Belgium, without consultation of the local population.

16. Leslie Gelb, 'Zelfbeschikking is Vaker een Vloek dan Zegen' ['Self-determination is More Often a Curse than a Blessing'], *de Volkskrant* (Amsterdam), 7 July 1992.

17. Ruth B. Russell, *A History of the United Nations Charter: the Role of the United States 1940–1945*, Washington, DC: Brookings Institution, 1958, p. 831.

18. Nowak, op. cit. (note 12), p. 9.

19. Vienna Declaration and Programme of Action, Adopted by the World Conference on Human Rights on 25 June 1993, Chapter I, par. 2.

20. Ibid.

21. Antonio Cassese, 'The Self-Determination of Peoples', in Louis Henkin (ed.), *The International Bill of Rights: the Covenant on Civil and Political Rights*, New York: Columbia University Press, 1981, pp. 96 ff.

22. Rosalyn Higgins, op. cit. (note 13), pp. 118–19.

23. UNGA Resolution 742 (VIII), 27 November 1953.

24. Rosalyn Higgins refers to the International Court of Justice in the case of the Western Sahara. But: 'Those instances were based either on the consideration that a certain population did not constitute a "people" entitled to self-determination or on the conviction that a consultation was totally unnecessary, in view of special circumstances.' (*ICJ Reports* (1975) 33, par. 59, as cited by Higgins, op. cit. (note 13), p. 119).

25. UNGA Resolution 2625 (XXV).

26. Nowak, op. cit. (note 12), p. 23.

27. Second Chamber of Parliament, 1978–79, 15 571, nos 1–2 (official English version).

28. Second Chamber of Parliament, 1992–93, 23 270, no. 1 [my translation from the Dutch].

29. Advisory Committee on Human Rights and Foreign Policy, *Collective Rights*, op. cit. (note 4), pp. 13–14 (official English version).

30. Even the 'African Charter on Human and *Peoples'* Rights' [italics supplied] does not contain a definition of the word. See also Aureliu Cristescu, *The Right to Self-Determination: Historical and Current Development on the Basis of United Nations Instruments*, UN Doc. E/CN.4/Sub.2/404/ Rev.1, pp. 39 ff.

31. Cf. Nowak, op. cit. (note 12), p. 21: 'The sole undisputed point is that *peoples living under colonial rule or comparable alien subjugation* are entitled to the right of self-determination.'

32. Martinez Cobo, *Study on the Problem of Discrimination against Indigenous Populations*, vol. 5 (UN Doc. E/CN.4/Sub.2/1986/7/Add.4, par. 379, cited in Julian Burger and Paul Hunt, 'Towards the International Protection of Indigenous Peoples' Rights', *Netherlands Quarterly of Human Rights*, vol. 12 (1994), p. 411.

33. 'Draft Declaration on the Rights of Indigenous Peoples', UN Doc.E/CN.4/ Sub.2/1993/29, pp. 50–60, reprinted in *Netherlands Quarterly of Human Rights*, vol. 12 (1994), pp. 471–9. Also, ILO Convention 169 is not very helpful in this regard, as the concept of 'people' to be defined is itself part of the definition. Indigenous peoples are described as follows: '(a) tribal peoples

in independent countries whose social, cultural and economic conditions distinguish them from other sections of the national community, and whose status is regulated wholly or partially by their own customs or traditions or by special laws or regulations; (b) peoples in independent countries who are regarded as indigenous on account of their descent from the populations which inhabited the country, or a geographical region to which the country belongs, at the time of conquest or colonisation or the establishment of present state boundaries and who, irrespective of their legal status, retain some or all of their own social, economic and cultural and political institutions' (as cited by Burger/Hunt, op. cit. (note 32), p. 411).

34. Ibid.
35. James Crawford (ed.), *The Rights of Peoples*, Oxford: Clarendon Press, 1988, p. 170.
36. *NRC Handelsblad* (Rotterdam), 5 January 1995 [my translation from the Dutch]. The European Council of Ministers did not go so far and limited itself to expressing its 'concern' about the developments in Chechnya (*de Volkskrant*, Amsterdam, 24 January 1995).
37. See Rachel Denbar, 'The Legacy of Abuse in Chechnya and OSCE Intervention', *Helsinki Monitor*, vol. 8 (1997), p. 62: 'The current legal status of Chechnya is undefined. Russian officials insist that Chechnya is undisputedly a subject of the Russian Federation and that Russian law must apply there; Chechen officials insist on the independence of Chechen government institutions (but are careful to state their willingness to cooperate with Russian governmental and legal bodies) and allow that Russian law may apply so long as it does not contradict Chechen law.'
38. UNGA Resolution 1514 (XV).
39. Higgins, op. cit. (note 13), p. 122.
40. CCPR/C/2/Rev.3, 12 May 1992. Higgins has made the point that this declaration is a limitation of the right of self-determination which is not mentioned in the UN Charter (R. Higgins, 'The United Nations Still a Force for Peace', *Modern Law Review*, vol. 52 (1989), p. 14.
41. Elisabeth Lijnzaad, *Reservations to UN Human Rights Treaties: Ratify and Ruin?* The Hague: T.M.C. Asser Instituut, 1994, p. 222. France indicated that the reservation attached conditions to the right of self-determination that were not provided in the UN Charter; Germany considered the reservation incompatible with the object and purpose of the Covenant; the Netherlands considered that attempts to limit the right of self-determination would seriously weaken its universally acceptable character.
42. Higgins, op. cit. (note 13), p. 116.
43. As quoted by McCorquodale, op. cit. (note 14), p. 857.

6 THE UNITED NATIONS ORGANS

1. This chapter is an adapted version of Chapter 5 of Peter R. Baehr and Leon Gordenker, *The United Nations at the End of the 1990s*, London: Macmillan, 1999.

2.   The best survey of the role of the United Nations in the field of human rights is Philip Alston (ed.), *The United Nations and Human Rights: a Critical Appraisal*, Oxford: Clarendon Press, 1992.

3.   On the basis of article 68 of the UN Charter: 'The Economic and Social Council shall set up commissions in economic and social fields *and for the promotion of human rights*, and such other commissions as may be required for the performance of its functions' [italics supplied]. See further, Howard B. Tolley Jr, *The U.N. Commission on Human Rights*, Boulder & London: Westview Press, 1987; Philip Alston, 'The Commission on Human Rights', in Alston, op. cit. (note 2), pp. 126–210.

4.   If a majority of its members so decides, the Commission can also meet in special session. This has happened in 1992, when it met twice in special session to discuss the situation in the former Yugoslavia. In May 1994, the Commission met in special session with regard to Rwanda.

5.   In 1997, the then existing UN Human Rights Centre was joined with the Office of the High Commissioner of Human Rights.

6.   See Asbjørn Eide, 'The Sub-Commission on Prevention of Discrimination and Protection of Minorities', in Alston, op. cit. (note 2), pp. 211–64.

7.   See David Weissbrodt, Mayna Gómez and Bret Thiele, 'A Review of the Fifty-Second Session of the United Nations Sub-Commission on the Promotion and Protection of Human Rights', *Netherlands Quarterly of Human Rights*, vol. 18 (December 2000), pp. 545–63.

8.   Karl Josef Partsch, 'The Committee on the Elimination of Racial Discrimination', in Alston, op. cit. (note 2), pp. 339–68.

9.   See Alston, op. cit. (note 2), pp. 473–508. See further, Kitty Arambulo, 'Improving Supervision of the International Convenant on Economic, Social and Cultural Rights', in Mielle Bulterman, Aart Hendriks, Jacqueline Smith (eds), *To Baehr in Our Minds: Essays on Human Rights from the Heart of the Netherlands*, SIM Special No. 21, Utrecht: SIM, 1998, pp. 9–23.

10. See Chapter 4.

11. See Dominic McColdrick, *The Human Rights Committee: Its Role in the Development of the International Covenant on Civil and Political Rights*, Oxford: Clarendon Press, 1991; Torkel Opsahl, 'The Human Rights Committee', in Alston, op. cit. (note 2), pp. 369–443.

12. See Sarah Joseph, 'New Procedures Concerning the Human Rights Committee's Examination of State Reports', *Netherlands Quarterly of Human Rights*, vol. 13 (1995), pp. 5–23; Ineke Boerefijn, *The Reporting Procedure under the Covenant on Civil and Political Rights: Practice and Procedures of the Human Rights Committee*, Antwerp/Groningen/Oxford: Intersentia/Hart, 1999.

13. See Markus G. Schmidt, 'Individual Human Rights Complaints Procedure Based on UN Treaties and the Need for Reform', *International and Comparative Law Quarterly*, vol. 41 (1992), pp. 645–90.

14. Twenty-five of the 26 general comments that have been issued so far have been collected by the Swedish Raoul Wallenberg Institute: *General Comments or Recommendations adopted by the United Nations Treaty Bodies, volume 1: Human Rights Committee*, Lund: Raoul Wallenberg Institute, 1997.

15. See William A. Schabas, *The Abolition of the Death Penalty in International Law*, Cambridge: Grotius, 1993. For the death penalty, see further, Chapter 3.
16. See Chapter 3.
17. See Laura Reanda, 'The Commission on the Status of Women', in Alston, op. cit. (note 2), pp. 265–303.
18. See Roberta Jackson, 'The Committee on the Elimination of Discrimination against Women', in Alston, op. cit. (note 2), pp. 444–72.
19. See Chapter 3.
20. See Thomas Hammerberg, 'The UN Convention on the Rights of the Child – and How to Make It Work', *Human Rights Quarterly*, vol. 12 (February 1990), pp. 97–105; Cynthia Price Cohen, Stuart N. Hart, and Susan M. Kosloske, 'Monitoring the United Nations Convention on the Rights of the Child: the Challenge of Information Management', *Human Rights Quarterly*, vol. 18 (May 1996), pp. 439–71.
21. See Chapter 3. See also Amnesty International, 'The Draft Optional Protocol to the Convention against Torture', AI INDEX: IOR 51/01/96 (July 1996).
22. See Andrew Clapham, 'Creating the High Commissioner for Human Rights: the Outside Story', *European Journal of International Law*, vol. 5 (1994), pp. 556–68.
23. See, for example, Amnesty International, *Agenda for a New United Nations High Commissioner for Human Rights*, AI INDEX: IOR 40/08/97.
24. See, for example, Advisory Committee on Human Rights and Foreign Policy, *UN Supervision of Human Rights*, advisory report No. 22, The Hague: Ministry of Foreign Affairs, 1996. This advisory report has been adopted by the Netherlands Government and submitted to other governments as a UN document: 'Human Rights Questions: Human Rights Situations and Reports of Special Rapporteurs and Special Representatives', UNGA A/52/64, 29 January 1997.
25. See Virginia Leary, 'Lessons from the Experience of the International Labour Organisation', in Alston, op. cit. (note 2), pp. 580–619.
26. See Peter R. Baehr, 'The General Assembly: Negotiating the Convention on Torture', in David P. Forsythe (ed.), *The United Nations in the World Political Economy: Essays in Honor of Leon Gordenker*, London: Macmillan, 1989, pp. 36–53. See also J. Herman Burgers, 'An Arduous Delivery: the United Nations Convention against Torture', in Johan Kaufmann (ed.), *Effective Negotiation: Case Studies in Conference Diplomacy*, Dordrecht: Kluwer, 1989, pp. 45–52. See further, Chapter 3.

7   REGIONAL SUPERVISORY MECHANISMS

1. For recent developments in the field of human rights, see the periodic surveys in *Netherlands Quarterly of Human Rights*.
2. The term 'European' is not used in the title of the Convention. In practice, however, it is always referred to as the *European* Convention on Human Rights.

3. The original European Commission of Human Rights and the Court merged in November 1998, when the Eleventh Protocol entered into force. See: 'Protocol No. 11 to the Convention for the Protection of Human Rights and Fundamental Freedoms, Restructuring the Control Machinery Established Thereby', *Netherlands Quarterly of Human Rights*, vol. 12 (1994), pp. 227–37; K. De Vey Mestdagh, 'Reform of the European Convention on Human Rights in a Changing Europe', in Rick Lawson and Matthijs de Blois (eds), *The Dynamics of the Protection of Human Rights in Europe*, Dordrecht /Boston/London: Martinus Nijhoff, 1994, pp. 337–60; Yvonne Klerk, 'Protocol No. 11 to the European Convention for Human Rights: a Drastic Revision of the Supervisory Mechanism under the ECHR', *Netherlands Quarterly of Human Rights*, vol. 14 (1996), pp. 35–46.

4. See Leo Zwaak, 'A Friendly Settlement in the European Inter-State Complaints against Turkey', *SIM Newsletter*, No. 13 (February 1986), pp. 44–8. This also appeared when the European Committee for the Prevention of Torture took in 1992 the unusual step – that is without cooperation by the Turkish Government – to publish its report which showed that torture and other forms of inhuman treatment were taking place in Turkish prisons and police cells. In December 1996, the Committee published another such report. See European Committee for the Prevention of Torture and Inhuman and Degrading Treatment or Punishment, *Public Statement on Turkey*, adopted on 15 December 1992; *Public Statement on Turkey*, CPT/Inf(96)34, adopted on 6 December 1996. Turkey was one of five countries which received particular attention by Amnesty International in its recent reports to the UN Commission on Human Rights: *1997 UN Commission on Human Rights – 50 Years Old*, AI INDEX: IOR 41/01/97, January 1997 and: *1998 UN Commission on Human Rights – Building on Past Achievements*, AI INDEX: IOR 41/01/98, January 1998.

5. Before the Eleventh Protocol entered into force (see note 3), it was a part-time function.

6. See R.A. Lawson, H.G. Schermers (eds), *Leading Cases of the European Court of Human Rights*, Nijmegen: Ars Aequi Libri, 1997.

7. See D.J. Harris, M. O'Boyle, C. Warbrick, *Law of the European Convention on Human Rights*, London/Dublin/Edinburgh: Butterworths, 1995, p. 33, which also stresses the problems of language, distance, costs and deficiencies of procedure.

8. Lawson and Schermers, op. cit. (note 6), p. xxxiii. The remaining cases were still pending.

9. Ibid., p. xxxix.

10. Klerk, op. cit. (note 3), pp. 44–6.

11. A separate problem is the question whether the legal systems and the political situation in countries such as the Russian Federation, Ukraine, Romania and Croatia are ready for application of the ECHR. Many observers doubt whether this is the case (see editorial comment in *Netherlands Quarterly of Human Rights*, vol. 12 (1994), p. 368 and vol. 14 (March 1996), pp. 3–4.

12. For recent developments in the field of human rights in the European Union, see the periodic surveys in *Netherlands Quarterly of Human Rights*.

13. Andrew Clapham begins his book on human rights and the European Community with the following quotation from Judge Pescatore: '[T]he builders of the European Communities thought too little about the legal foundations of their edifice and paid too little attention to the protection of the basic rights of the individual within the new European structure.' (Andrew Clapham, *Human Rights and the European Community: a Critical Overview*, Baden-Baden: Nomos Verlagsgesellschaft, 1991, p. 7.)

14. Joint Declaration on Fundamental Rights by the European Parliament, the Council and the Commission of 5 April 1977 (OJ C 103/1); Declaration on Human Rights by the Ministers of Foreign Affairs in the Framework of European Political Cooperation and the Council, 21 July 1986 (Bull. EC 7/8–1986), 2.4.4); Declaration on Human Rights of the European Council in Luxembourg (28 and 29 June 1991), in C. Duparc, *The European Community and Human Rights*, Office for Official Publications of the European Communities, Luxembourg 1993, pp. 48–51.

15. Treaty on European Union, Title V, Article J.1.

16. During the 1997 session of the UN Commission on Human Rights, there was an utter failure, however, when there turned out to be no consensus among EU members on the introduction of a draft resolution on human rights in China. See further, Chapter 8.

17. Johannes van der Klaauw, 'European Union', *Netherlands Quarterly of Human Rights*, vol. 15 (1997), p. 210.

18. See for a similar conclusion about the human rights aspects of EU activities with reference to development cooperation: Karin Arts, *Integrating Human Rights into Development Cooperation: The Case of the Lomé Convention*, Ph.D. dissertation Free University (Amsterdam) 2000. See also: Mielle Bulterman, *Human Rights in the Treaty Relations of the European Community: Real Virtues or Virtual Reality?*, Antwerp/Groningen/Oxford: Intersentia/Hart, 2001.

19. See note 16 above.

20. For recent developments, see the periodic surveys in *Netherlands Quarterly of Human Rights* and *Helsinki Monitor*.

21. All former Soviet republics now belong to the OSCE.

22. See Arie Bloed, 'The Human Dimension of the OSCE: More Words than Deeds?' *Helsinki Monitor*, vol. 6 (1995), pp. 23–9.

23. See Arie Bloed, 'OSCE', *Netherlands Quarterly of Human Rights*, vol. 13 (1995), p. 182: 'The change of the name is intended to clarify the view of the participating States that the CSCE/OSCE is a major security institution at the European continent. However, it is doubtful whether that purpose is met, in particular, because the character of the institution has not been changed in any way.'

24. See Michel Mahalka, 'A Marriage of Convenience: the OSCE and Russia in Nagorny-Karabakh and Chechnya', *Helsinki Monitor*, vol. 7 (1996), pp. 13–28; Rachel Denbar, 'The Legacy of Abuse in Chechnya and OSCE Intervention', *Helsinki Monitor*, vol. 8 (1997), pp. 59–74; Arie Bloed, 'OSCE and Nagorno-Karabakh', *Helsinki Monitor*, vol. 8 (1997), pp. 91–3.

25.   See Arie Bloed, 'OSCE', *Netherlands Quarterly of Human Rights*, vol. 14 (1996), p. 470.

26.   See Rob Zaagman and Joanne Thorburn, *The Role of the High Commissioner on National Minorities in OSCE Conflict Prevention*, The Hague: Foundation for Inter-Ethnic Relations, June 1997.

27.   It should be added that the mandate of the High Commissioner explicitly excludes dealing with minorities where there are 'organized deeds of terrorism'. These were excluded at the time at the request of Great Britain and France, which did not want any involvement with the situation in Northern Ireland and the Basque country, respectively. Moreover, the French government is of the opinion that, because of Article 2 of the French Constitution ('France is a republic, indivisible, secular, democratic, and social. It shall ensure the equality of all citizens before the law, without distinction of origin, race, or religion. It shall respect all beliefs') it has no minorities. The British human rights expert Nigel Rodley has rightly questioned the logic of that reasoning (see Nigel Rodley, 'Conceptual Problems in the Protection of Minorities: International Legal Developments', *Human Rights Quarterly*, vol. 17 (1995), pp. 51–2).

28.   For recent developments in the field of human rights, see the periodic surveys in *Netherlands Quarterly of Human Rights*.

29.   See Cecilia Medina Quiroga, *The Battle of Human Rights: Gross, Systematic Violations and the Inter-American System*, Dordrecht: Martinus Nijhoff, 1988; Cecilia Medina, 'The Inter-American Commission on Human Rights and the Inter-American Court of Human Rights: Reflections on a Joint Venture', *Human Rights Quarterly*, vol. 12 (1990), pp. 439–64; Tom Farer, 'The Rise of the Inter-American Human Rights Regime: No Longer a Unicorn, Not Yet an Ox', *Human Rights Quarterly*, vol. 19 (1997), pp. 510–46.

30.   For the results of interviews with current and former judges of the Court, see Lynda E. Frost, 'The Evolution of the Inter-American Court of Human Rights: Reflections of Present and Former Judges', *Human Rights Quarterly*, vol. 14 (1992), pp. 171–205.

31.   Farer, op. cit. (note 29), p. 546.

32.   They share this position with the Bahamas, Belize, Cuba, Guyana and the microstates Saint Kitts and Nevis, Saint Lucia, and Saint Vincent and the Grenadines.

33.   For recent developments in the field of human rights in Africa, see the periodic surveys in *Netherlands Quarterly of Human Rights*.

34.   Wolfgang Benedek, 'The African Charter and Commission on Human and Peoples' Rights: How to Make It More Effective', *Netherlands Quarterly of Human Rights*, vol. 11 (1993), pp. 25–40.

35.   Richard N. Kiwanuka, 'The Meaning of "People" in the African Charter on Human and Peoples' Rights', *American Journal of International Law*, vol. 82 (1988), pp. 80–101.

36.   See Evelyn Ama Ankumah, *The African Commission on Human and Peoples' Rights: Practice and Procedures*, The Hague: Martinus Nijhoff, 1996.

37.   Claude E. Welch Jr, 'The African Commission on Human and Peoples' Rights: a Five-Year Report and Assessment,' *Human Rights Quarterly*, vol. 14 (1992), pp. 44 and 49.

38. In 1995, it met for the second time in special session to discuss the human rights situation in Nigeria and in Burundi (see Susanne Malström and Gerd Oberleitner, 'Africa', *Netherlands Quarterly of Human Rights*, vol. 14 (1996), p. 94).

39. Rachel Murray, 'Decisions by the African Commission on Individual Communications under the African Charter on Human and Peoples' Rights', *International and Comparative Law Quarterly*, vol. 46 (1997), pp. 412–34.

40. See Wolfgang Benedek and Gerd Oberleitner, 'Africa', *Netherlands Quarterly of Human Rights*, vol. 14 (1996), p. 226.

41. Felice D. Gaer, 'First Fruits: Reporting by States under the African Charter on Human and Peoples' Rights', *Netherlands Quarterly of Human Rights*, vol. 10 (1992), pp. 29–42; Wolfgang Benedek, 'Enforcement of Human and Peoples' Rights in Africa: the Communication System and State Reporting under the African Charter', in Jacqueline Smith and Leo Zwaak (eds), *International Protection of Human Rights*, Utrecht: SIM Special No. 15, pp. 23–43. In 1995, the Commission had to remind 28 states parties of their obligation to submit their first report. Some were already more than twelve years overdue (see Malmström and Oberleitner, op. cit. (note 38), p. 93).

42. During the eighteenth session of the Commission in October 1995, the English speaking members had no access to the report of Tunisia, as there were no facilities to have it translated in time from the original French into English (see Malmström and Oberleitner, op. cit. (note 38), p. 94). The same problem occurred in 1996, when the report of Mauretania was to be discussed (see Gerd Oberleitner, 'Africa', *Netherlands Quarterly of Human Rights*, vol. 15 (1997), p. 221).

43. See Oberleitner, op. cit. (note 42), pp. 218–23.

8 FOREIGN POLICY

1. This chapter is based on Chapters 3 and 4 of my *The Role of Human Rights in Foreign Policy*, London: Macmillan, 2nd edn, 1996, pp. 23–47 and my article 'Problems of Aid Conditionality: the Netherlands and Indonesia', *Third World Quarterly*, vol. 18 (1997), pp. 363–76.

2. Ministry of Foreign Affairs of the Kingdom of the Netherlands, *Human Rights and Foreign Policy*, Memorandum presented to the Lower House of the States General of the Kingdom of the Netherlands on 3 May 1979 by the Minister for Foreign Affairs and the Minister for Development Cooperation, 71 [official English version].

3. In its third Progress Note (1997) it speaks of one of the regular 'tracks' of foreign policy: 'Contacts with countries are considered to have many forms and one of these forms is a dialogue, in which human rights can be put at issue, if necessary. This putting at issue can happen at different levels, both

162 *Notes*

administratively and politically' (Second Chamber of Parliament, 1996–97, 25 300 No. 1, 9 April 1997, p. 7) [translated from the original Dutch].

4. Memorandum, op. cit. (note 2), p. 136.
5. See my 'Problems of Aid Conditionality', op. cit. (note 1).
6. Max van der Stoel, 'De Rechten van de Mens in de Oost–West betrekkingen' ['Human Rights in East–West Relations'], in Ph.P. Everts and J.L. Heldring (eds), *Nederland en de Rechten van de Mens*, Baarn: Anthos, 1981, p. 79 [translated from the original Dutch].
7. See Amnesty International, *Turkey: Student Campaigners Tortured and Imprisoned*, AI INDEX EUR 44/54/97, September 1997; *Turkey: the Colours of their Clothes – Parliamentary Deputies Serve 15 Years' Imprisonment for Expressions of their Kurdish Political Identity*, AI INDEX: EUR 44/85/97, December 1997; Article XIX, *State before Freedom: Media Repression in Turkey*, London, July 1998.
8. See Leo Zwaak, 'A Friendly Settlement in the European Inter-State Complaints against Turkey,' *SIM Newsletter*, No. 13, February 1986, pp. 44–8.
9. Ph. P. Everts (ed.), *Controversies at Home: Domestic Factors in the Foreign Policy of the Netherlands*, Dordrecht: Martinus Nijhoff, 1985.
10. See further, Marlies Glasius, 'Human Rights Conditionality Between the Netherlands and Indonesia: Two Cases Compared', in Mielle Bulterman, Aart Hendriks, Jacqueline Smith (eds), *To Baehr in Our Minds: Essays on Human Rights from the Heart of the Netherlands*, SIM Special No. 21, Utrecht: SIM, 1998, pp. 249–69.
11. Peer Baneke, *Nederland en de Indonesische Gevangenen* ['The Netherlands and the Indonesian Prisoners'], Amsterdam: Wiardi Beckman Stichting, 1983, p. 9.
12. Baneke, op. cit. (note 11), p. 11.
13. As late as August 1995, on the occasion of the celebration of the fiftieth anniversary of Indonesian independence, three prominent political prisoners were released, including former vice-prime minister Subandrio, who had been under arrest for 30 years.
14. See Hans Goderbauer, 'Indonesia and East Timor', in Bård Anders Andreassen, Theresa Swinehart (eds), *Human Rights in Developing Countries: Yearbook 1993*, Oslo: Nordic Human Rights Publications, 1993, p. 137.
15. This was the 'timebomb' which shortly afterwards would end Dutch–Indonesian development relations. See Nico G. Schulte Nordholt, 'Aid and Conditionality: the Case of Dutch–Indonesian Relationships', in Olav Stokke (ed.), *Aid and Political Conditionality*, London: Frank Cass, 1995, p. 153.
16. Schulte Nordholt, op. cit. (note 15), p. 153.
17. Press statement by the Indonesian government, 25 March 1992.
18. Peter Baehr, Hilde Selbervik and Arne Tostensen, 'Responses to Human Rights Criticism: Kenya–Norway and Indonesia–the Netherlands', in Peter Baehr, Hilde Hey, Jacqueline Smith, Theresa Swinehart (eds), *Human Rights in Developing Countries: Yearbook 1995*, The Hague/London/Boston: Kluwer Law International, 1995, pp. 64–94.
19. That was made evident, when in August 1995 no less than 50 high-ranking representatives of Dutch business firms – the largest delegation of its kind – visited Indonesia in the wake of Queen Beatrix's official visit.

20. E. Luard, *Human Rights and Foreign Policy*, Oxford: Pergamon Press, 1981, pp. 26–7.
21. Ibid., pp. 28–9.
22. UNGA Resolution 2625 (XXV).
23. Cf. Peter Malanczuk, *Humanitarian Intervention and the Legitimacy of the Use of Force*, Amsterdam: Het Spinhuis, 1993; Adam Roberts, 'Humanitarian War: Military Intervention and Human Rights', *International Affairs*, vol. 69, pp. 429–50; Nigel Rodley (ed.), *To Loose the Bands of Wickedness: International Intervention in Defence of Human Rights*, London: Brassey's, 1992.
24. Cf. Peter Malanczuk, 'The Kurdish Crisis and Allied Intervention in the Aftermath of the Second Gulf War', *European Journal of International Law*, vol. 2 (1991), pp. 114–32.
25. S/RES/688 (1991).
26. S/RES/733 (1992).
27. Michael Akehurst, 'Humanitarian Intervention', in Hedley Bull, *Intervention in World Politics*, Oxford: Clarendon Press, 1985, pp. 97–9.
28. R.J. Vincent, *Non-intervention and International Order*, Princeton NJ: Princeton University Press, 1974, p. 346.
29. Cf. Marc Bossuyt, 'Human Rights and Non-Intervention in Domestic Matters', *ICJ Review* 35 (1985), pp. 50–1.
30. *NRC Handelsblad* (Rotterdam), 8 January 1983 [translated from the original Dutch].

9   HOW TO DEAL WITH PAST VIOLATIONS

1. See Iain Guest, *Behind the Disappearances: Argentina's Dirty War against Human Rights and the United Nations*, Philadelphia: University of Pennsylvania Press, 1990, pp. 52 ff. See further, Chapter 3 above.
2. See Karl Josef Partsch, 'The Federal Republic of Germany', in Theo van Boven *et al.* (eds), 'Seminar on the Right to Restitutions, Compensation and Rehabilitation for Victims of Gross Violations of Human Rights and Fundamental Freedoms, 11–15 March 1992', *SIM Special*, No. 12 (Utrecht: SIM, 1992), p. 132.
3. *International Herald Tribune*, 1 October 1997.
4. Theodor Adorno, 'Wounded Nations, Broken Lives: Truth Commissions and War Tribunals', *Index on Censorship*, vol. 5 (1996), p. 112.
5. In France, the Gayssot Act was adopted, which penalizes the denial of Nazi war-crimes. This act was considered by the UN Human Rights Committee, with reference to the case involved, not to be a violation of freedom of expression (CCPR/C/58/D/550/1993, 16 December 1996, p. 15).
6. In August 1997, the Japanese Supreme Court condemned the Ministry of Education for having deleted references in history books to the killing of civilians by the Japanese military during the Second World War ('Japan Bars Censorship of Atrocities in Texts', *New York Times*, 30 August 1997). See also 'Japan War Veterans now Speak of the Unspeakable', *International Herald Tribune*, 8 October 1997.

7. *International Herald Tribune*, 27 January 1997.
8. See, for example, Jeri Laber and Invana Nizich, 'The War Crimes Tribunal for the Former Yugoslavia: Problems and Prospects', *The Fletcher Forum*, vol. 18 (1994), pp. 8–9; David P. Forsythe, 'Politics and the International Tribunal for the Former Yugoslavia', *Criminal Law Forum*, vol. 5 (1994), pp. 415 ff. Forsythe quotes the former US diplomat Morris Abrams as follows: 'It is a very tough call whether to point the finger or try to negotiate with people. As a lawyer or as a politician or as a statesman, I would also like to stop the slaughter, bring it to a halt. You have two things that are in real conflict here [...] I don't know the proper mix.' See further, Payam Akhavan, 'The Yugoslav Tribunal at a Crossroads; the Dayton Peace Agreements and Beyond', *Human Rights Quarterly*, vol. 18 (1996), pp. 267–74; David P. Forsythe, 'International Criminal Courts: a Political View', *Netherlands Quarterly of Human Rights*, vol. 15 (1997), p. 11; Payam Akhavan, 'Justice in The Hague, Peace in the Former Yugoslavia? A Commentary on the United Nations War Crimes Tribunal', *Human Rights Quarterly*, vol. 20 (1998), pp. 737–816.
9. Luc Huyse, 'Justice after Transition: On the Choices Successor Elites Make in Dealing with the Past', *Law and Social Inquiry*, vol. 20 (1995), p. 65.
10. Daniel Joel Goldhagen, *Hitler's Willing Executioners: Ordinary Germans and the Holocaust*, London: Abacus, 1997.
11. Forsythe, op. cit. (note 8), p. 13.
12. 'The General Framework Agreement for Peace in Bosnia and Herzegovina', *Netherlands Quarterly of Human Rights*, vol. 14 (1996), pp. 102–10.
13. On the other hand, as was not the case with the Yugoslav Tribunal, most of the suspects in Rwanda are already in detention and the states in question have in principle agreed to cooperate. This may mean that the Rwanda Tribunal may be able to work faster than its counterpart on Yugoslavia.
14. *Index on Censorship*, op. cit. (note 4), p. 39.
15. Priscilla B. Hayner, 'Fifteen Truth Commissions – 1974 to 1994: a Comparative Study', *Human Rights Quarterly*, vol. 16 (1994), p. 600. See also Michelle Parlevliet, 'Considering Truth: Dealing with a Legacy of Gross Human Rights Violations', *Netherlands Quarterly of Human Rights*, vol. 16 (1998), pp. 141–74, Priscilla B. Hayner, *Unspeakable Truths: Confronting State Terror and Atrocity*, New York and London; Routledge, 2001.
16. *Truth Commissions: an Interdisciplinary Discussion held at Harvard Law School in May 1996*, Cambridge MA: Harvard Law School Human Rights Program, 1997, p. 50.
17. Hayner, op. cit. (note 15), p. 607.
18. *Report submitted by Mr. Manfred Nowak, expert member of the Working Group on Enforced or Involuntary Disappearances, responsible for the special process, pursuant to paragraph 4 of Commission resolution 1995/35*, E/CN.4/1996/36, 4 March 1996. The appointed expert, Dr Manfred Nowak, felt forced to resign in March 1997 by way of protest against the lack of will of the states concerned to help him carry out his mandate. See 'United Nations Expert on Missing Persons in Former Yugoslavia Resigns', UN Document, HR/CN/780, Press release, 2 April 1997.
19. *Index on Censorship*, op. cit. (note 4), p. 114.
20. Ibid.

21. See, for example, the following statement by Ntsiki Biko (widow of the slain South African anti-Apartheid activist Steve Biko):

     To me it is an insult [to be asked to testify before the South African Commission on Truth and Reconciliation], because all that is needed is to have the perpetrators taken to a proper court of justice. . . . I doubt very much whether they can convince me that this Truth Commission is going to bring us reconciling: one would think of reconciling after justice, but justice must be done first.
     It can never be easy. To me, really, it is just opening the wounds for nothing. Because these people are going to go to the Commission – I suppose they have applied or their names have been taken. But if they go there, are they going to tell the truth? Or are they going to lie so they will get amnesty? (*Index on Censorship*, op. cit. (note 4), p. 68).

22. Cf. Daan Bronkhorst, *Truth and Reconciliation: Obstacles and Opportunities for Human Rights*, Amsterdam: Amnesty International, 1995, pp. 26–7; idem, 'Naming Names', *Netherlands Quarterly of Human Rights*, vol. 16 (1998), pp. 457–74.

23. Therefore Rhoda Howard was right when she claimed that torture was not 'inhuman'. See Rhoda Howard, 'Dignity, Community and Human Rights', in Abdullahi An-Na'im (ed.), *Human Rights in Cross-Cultural Perspectives: a Quest for Consensus*, Philadelphia: University of Pennsylvania Press, 1992, p. 89.

24. *Index on Censorship*, op. cit. (note 4), p. 113.

10 NON-GOVERNMENTAL ORGANIZATIONS

1. This chapter is based on my 'Mobilization of the Conscience of Mankind: Conditions of Effectiveness of Human Rights NGOs', in Erik Denters and Nico Schrijver (eds), *Reflections on International Law in the Low Countries in Honour of Paul de Waart*, The Hague/Boston/London: Martinus Nijhoff Publishers, 1998, pp. 135–55.

2. Cf. Peter R. Baehr, 'Human Rights Organizations and the UN: a Tale of Two Worlds', in Dimitris Bourantonis and Jarrod Wiener (eds), *The United Nations in the New World Order*, London: Macmillan, 1995, p. 171; Leon Gordenker and Thomas G. Weiss, 'Pluralizing Global Governance: Analytical Approaches and Dimensions', in Thomas Weiss and Leon Gordenker, *NGOs, the UN, and Global Governance*, Boulder/London: Lynne Rienner, 1996, pp. 18–21; Dianne Otto, 'Nongovernmental Organizations in the United Nations System: the Emerging Role of International Civil Society', *Human Rights Quarterly*, vol. 18 (1996), pp. 100–13.

3. Manfred Nowak and Ingeborg Schwarz, 'The Contribution of Non-Governmental Organizations', in Manfred Nowak (ed.), *World Conference on Human Rights*, Vienna: Manzsche Verlags- und Universitätsbuchhandlung, 1994, p. 1.

4. GONGOs: government-organized non-governmental organizations, which achieved notoriety during the Cold War because they owed their very existence and entire financial support to communist governments in

the Soviet bloc or authoritarian ones in the Third World. QUANGOs: quasi-nongovernmental organizations: many Nordic and Canadian NGOs and a handful of US ones, as well as the ICRC receive the bulk of their resources from public funds. DONGOs: donor-organized non-governmental organizations are also distinguished by their source of funds, from donor governments or intergovernmental organizations to promote or to carry out tasks established by their financial backers (Weiss and Gordenker, op. cit. (note 2), pp. 20–1). This list is by no means exhaustive, as indicated by the following additions by a Japanese scholar: AGOs: anti-government organizations, TRANGOs: transnational NGOs; GRINGOs: government regulated and initiated NGOs; BINGOs: business and industry NGOs; DODONGOs: donor-dominated NGOs; ODANGOs: ODA-financed NGOs; and FLAMINGOs: flashy minded NGOs representing the rich (Tatsuro Kunugi, 'The United Nations and Civil Society – NGOs Working towards the 21st Century', unpublished paper).

5. Laurie S. Wiseberg, 'Protecting Human Rights Activists and NGOs: What Can Be Done?' *Human Rights Quarterly*, vol. 13 (1991), p. 529. She refers to Henry J. Steiner, *Diverse Partners: Non-Governmental Organizations in the Human Rights Movement, the Report of a Retreat of Human Rights Activists*, Cambridge Mass.: Harvard Law School Human Rights Program and Human Rights Internet, 1990, pp. 5–15.
6. Gordenker and Weiss, op. cit. (note 2), p. 24.
7. P. Comeau, 'Mood is Positive as the UN Begins Review of NGO Status', *Human Rights Tribune*, September/October 1994, p. 26.
8. Amnesty International, which aspires to have national sections all over the world, thus being truly 'international', has been trying for many years to persuade international news agencies to delete the affix 'the London-based human rights organization'. So far, however, with little success.
9. See Ineke Boerefijn, 'Towards a Strong System of Supervision: the Human Rights Committee's Role in Reforming the Reporting Procedure under Article 40 of the Covenant on Civil and Political Rights', *Human Rights Quarterly*, vol. 17 (1995), p. 784.
10. Ibid., p. 785.
11. Felice D. Gaer, 'Reality Check: Human Rights NGOs Confront Governments at the UN', in Weiss and Gordenker, op. cit. (note 2), p. 56.
12. Ibid., p. 55.
13. For a useful survey of various kinds of government responses see Stanley Cohen, 'Government Responses to Human Rights Reports: Claims, Denials and Counterclaims', *Human Rights Quarterly*, vol. 18 (1996), pp. 517–43.
14. Antonio Donini, 'The Bureaucracy and the Free Spirits: Stagnation and Innovation in the Relationship between the UN and NGOs', in Weiss and Gordenker, op. cit. (note 2), p. 86.
15. Alston has remarked on the permanent tension between governments and NGOs: 'Despite the fact that NGOs are indispensable to the effective functioning of the [UN Human Rights] Commission, their position will never be accepted more than grudgingly by the states that make up the Commission. If it were otherwise, it would be safe to say that NGOs were not behaving as they should: in an informed, independent, critical,

and uncompromising manner.' (Philip Alston, 'The Commission on Human Rights', in Alston (ed.), *The United Nations and Human Rights*, Oxford: Clarendon Press, 1992, pp. 203–4.) However, Weiss and Gordenker suggest that the decline of oppressive regimes and the rise of democracy mainly since the end of the Cold War 'has tempered the former automatic hostility by governments toward the activities of local and international NGOs. Previously, NGO–government relationships were often ones of benign neglect at best, or of suspicion and outright hostility at worst' (Weiss and Gordenker, op. it. (note 2), p. 30).

16. J. Herman Burgers, 'Dutch Nongovernmental Organizations and Foreign Policy in the Field of Human Rights', in P.J. van Krieken and Ch.O. Pannenborg (eds), *Liber Akkerman: In- and Outlaws in War*, Apeldoorn/ Antwerpen: MAKLU Publishers, 1992, p. 168.

17. Victoria Berry and Allan McChesney, 'Human Rights and Foreign Policy-Making', in Robert O. Matthews and Cranford Pratt (eds), *Human Rights in Canadian Foreign Policy*, Kingston and Montreal: McGill-Queen's University Press, 1988, p. 60; John W. Foster, 'The UN Commission on Human Rights', in ibid., pp. 94–7.

18. Weiss and Gordenker, op. cit. (note 2), p. 36.

19. The pun is lost in translation: 'Knowledge is power, but acquaintances give even more power.'

20. Otto, op. cit. (note 2), p. 112, note 25. See also: Marc Nerfin, 'Neither Prince nor Merchant Citizen – An Introduction to the Third System', in Krishna Ahooja-Patel *et al.* (eds), *World Economy in Transition*, Oxford: Pergamon Press, 1986, p. 47; Theo van Boven, Statement at the Occasion of the Presentation of the Right Livelihood Honorary Award, Stockholm 1985: 'In the third system we find groups and organizations that defend the human factor and advocate a peoples oriented approach instead of relying on domination by power, strategies of deterrence and the law of force [...] Peace movements, environmental activists and numerous groups and organizations that expose violations of human rights belong to this movement, as well as women's organizations and defenders of the rights of minorities and of indigenous populations.' (Theodoor van Boven, 'Human Rights', in Tom Woodhouse (ed.), *People and Planet: Alternative Nobel Prize Speeches*, Hartland, Bideford, 1987, pp. 180–1.)

21. Amnesty International has members in more than 160 countries and territories, more than one million fee-paying members in sections of which more than 100 000 are active. (www.web.amnesty.org).

22. A. Fowler, 'The Role of NGOs in Changing State–Society Relations: Perspectives from Eastern and Southern Africa', *Development Policy Review*, vol. 9 (1991), p. 67 as quoted by Peter Uvin, 'Scaling Up the Grassroots and Scaling Down the Summit: the Relations Between Third World NGOs and the UN', in Weiss and Gordenker, op. cit. (note 2), p. 169. Fowler concludes: 'Maintaining accountability to its grassroots constituency while simultaneously building competencies and credibility with decision-makers is perhaps the overriding challenge facing NGOs that would influence policy.' (Uvin, pp. 169–70).

23.   Resolution 1996/31, 49th plenary meeting, 25 July 1996. In February
       1993, the ECOSOC established an open-ended working group to update,
       if necessary, its arrangements for consultation with NGOs and to introduce
       coherent rules to regulate the participation of NGOs in an international
       conference organized by the UN. Otto, op. cit. (note 2), pp. 120–2, lists
       the reasons for this review. See for a discussion of the newly adopted
       rules, Laurie S. Wiseberg, 'Resolution 1296 Revised: a Done Deal on
       Consultative Status, not Ideal but a Major Improvement', *Human Rights
       Tribune*, August/September 1996, p. 810.
24.   ECOSOC Resolution 1996/31, par. 12.
25.   Weiss and Gordenker, op. cit. (note 2), p. 219.
26.   Ibid.
27.   Statute of Amnesty International, as amended by the 23rd International
       Council, meeting in Capetown, South Africa, 12–19 December 1997,
       Article 3.
28.   Ibid., Art. 13.
29.   Cf. Peter R. Baehr, 'Amnesty International and its Self-Imposed Lim-
       ited Mandate,' *Netherlands Quarterly of Human Rights*, vol. 12 (1994),
       pp. 18–19.
30.   Otto, op. cit. (note 2), p. 138.
31.   Ibid.
32.   Weiss and Gordenker, op. cit. (note 2), p. 28.
33.   Cyril Ritchie, 'Coordinate? Cooperate? Harmonise? NGO Policy and
       Operational Coalitions', in Weiss and Gordenker, op. cit. (note 2),
       p. 181.
34.   Cf. Peter Uvin, op. cit. (note 22), p. 166. Falk has called such meetings
       'counter-conferences' (Richard Falk, 'The Global Promise of Social Move-
       ments: Explorations at the Edge of Time', *Alternatives*, vol. 12 (1987),
       p. 187, as quoted by Otto, op. cit. (note 2), p. 120).
35.   Ritchie, op. cit. (note 33), p. 183; see also Nowak and Schwarz, op. cit.
       (note 3), p. 7.
36.   Cf. Gaer, op. cit. (note 11), p. 59.
37.   Among these were: Albertina Sisulu, President of the Women's League of
       the African National Congress; Ibrahima Fall, Director of the UN Centre
       of Human Rights; Adama Dieng, Secretary-General of the International
       Commission of Jurists; and Nobel Prize-Winner Adolfo Perez Esquivel.
       However, among the attending NGOs the atmosphere was not always
       serene, as appeared when a number of Latin American representatives
       succeeded in shouting down former President Jimmy Carter, when he tried
       to deliver his address. In the somewhat euphemistic rendering in the NGO
       Newsletter relating to the World Conference, Carter was 'prevented by a
       number of NGO representatives to effectively communicate his message
       to the NGO community' (Nowak and Schwarz, op. cit. (note 3), p. 224).
38.   Gaer, op. cit. (note 11), p. 58.
39.   Nowak and Schwarz, op. cit. (note 3), p. 8.
40.   Personal communication from Laurie Wiseberg.
41.   'Time pressures at the 1995 Commission on Human Rights led its
       Malaysian chair to reduce by half the speaking time of all participants –
       governments and NGOs alike. Some governments argue that this should

diminish NGO "speechifying" in favour of on-the-record debate and discussion among member-states.' (Gaer, op. cit. (note 11), p. 64.)

42. Gaer, op. cit. (note 11), p. 64.
43. Op. cit. (note 23), par. 9.
44. Nowak and Schwarz, op. cit. (note 3), p. 11.
45. Ritchie, op. cit. (note 33), p. 186.
46. See James Henke, *Human Rights Now! The Official Book of the Concerts for Human Rights Foundation World Tour*, London: Bloomsbury, 1988, p. 16. At the occasion of the London concert, pop-star Bruce Springsteen commented: 'I think people come out to see the rock show, to dance and have fun. But if you reach a small percent, if you reach just one person, you've done something.' (*New York Times*, 3 September 1988.)
47. Reebok Athletic Shoe Corporation.
48. Cf. Martha Alter Chen, 'Engendering World Conferences: the International Women's Movement and the UN', in Weiss and Gordenker, op. cit. (note 2), p. 143.
49. Sikkink has rightly called attention to the importance of international human rights issue-networks. The diverse entities that make up the international human rights issue-network include parts of IGOs at both the international and regional levels, international NGOs on human rights, domestic NGOs on human rights and private foundations (Kathryn Sikkink, 'Human Rights, Principled Issue-Networks, and Sovereignty in Latin America', *International Organization*, vol. 47 (1993), pp. 411–41).
50. See further, Esther M. van den Berg, *The Influence of Domestic NGOs on Dutch Human Rights Policy: Case Studies on South Africa, Namibia, Indonesia and East Timor*, Antwerp/Groningen/Oxford: Intersentia/Hart, 2001.

11   CONCLUDING OBSERVATIONS

1. She seems to have made a start in this direction by her critical remarks about the human rights situation in Rwanda and Algeria. See 'Algeria Accuses UN Human Rights Commissioner of Exceeding Her Powers,' *BBC Summary of World Broadcasts*, 8 November 1997. See also 'Statement by Mary Robinson, UN High Commissioner for Human Rights', 52nd session of the General Assembly of the United Nations, Third Committee, 14 November 1997.
2. See Nicola Jägers, 'Transnational Corporations and Human Rights', in Mielle Bulterman, Aart Hendriks, Jacqueline Smith (eds), *To Baehr in Our Minds: Essays on Human Rights from the Heart of the Netherlands*, SIM Special No. 21, Utrecht: SIM, 1998, pp. 71–85.
3. UNHCR mentions 22 million refugees and an estimated 25 million displaced persons (2000).

Bibliography

This is a list of important studies on human rights in English. The notes to the separate chapters contain more detailed references

Alston, Philip (ed.), *The United Nations and Human Rights*, Oxford: Clarendon Press, 1992.

Alston, Philip (ed.), *The EU and Human Rights*, Oxford: Oxford University Press, 1999.

An-Na'im, Abdullahi Ahmed (ed.), *Human Rights in Cross-Cultural Perspectives: a Quest for Consensus*, Philadelphia: University of Pennsylvania Press, 1992.

An-Na'im, Abdullahi Ahmed, Francis M. Deng (eds), *Human Rights in Africa: Cross-Cultural Perspectives*, Washington, DC: Brookings Institution, 1990.

Baehr, P.R., *The Role of Human Rights in Foreign Policy*, London: Macmillan (– now Palgrave), 2nd edn, 1996.

Baehr, Peter R., Cees Flinterman and Mignon Senders (eds), *Innovation and Inspiration: Fifty Years of the Universal Declaration of Human Rights*, Amsterdam: Royal Netherlands Academy of Arts and Sciences, 1999.

Baehr, Peter R., Fried van Hoof, Liu Nanlai, Tao Zhenghua, Jacqueline Smith (eds), *Human Rights: Chinese and Dutch Perspectives*, The Hague/London/Boston: Martinus Nijhoff Publishers, 1996.

Banton, Michael, *International Action against Racial Discrimination*, Oxford: Clarendon Press, 1996.

Berting, Jan *et al.* (eds), *Human Rights in a Pluralist World: Individuals and Collectivities*, Westport/London: Meckler, 1990.

Boven, Theo van, *People Matter: Views on International Human Rights Policy*, Amsterdam: Meulenhof, 1982.

Bronkhorst, Daan, *Truth and Reconciliation: Obstacles and Opportunities for Human Rights*, Amsterdam: Amnesty International, 1995.

Buergenthal, Thomas, *International Human Rights*, St Paul, Minnesota: West Publishing Company, 1988.

Bulterman, Mielle, Aart Hendriks, Jacqueline Smith (eds), *To Baehr in Our Minds: Essays on Human Rights from the Heart of the Netherlands*, SIM Special No. 21, Utrecht: SIM, 1998.

Burgers, J.H., H. Danelius, *The United Nations Convention against Torture: a Handbook on the Convention against Torture and Other Cruel, Inhuman or Degrading Treatment or Punishment*, Dordrecht: Martinus Nijhoff Publishers, 1988.

Cassese, Antonio, *Human Rights in a Changing World*, Cambridge: Polity Press, 1990.

Castermans-Holleman, Monique, Fried van Hoof, Jacqueline Smith (eds), *The Role of the Nation-State in the 21st Century: Human Rights, International Organisations and Foreign Policy. Essays in Honour of Peter Baehr*, The Hague/Boston/London: Kluwer Law International, 1998.

Chowdhury, Subrata Roy, Erik M.G. Denters, Paul J.I.M. de Waart (eds), *The Right to Development in International Law*, Dordrecht/Boston/London: Martinus Nijhoff, 1992.

Clapham, Andrew, *Human Rights and the European Community: a Critical Overview*, Baden-Baden: Nomos Verlagsgesellschaft, 1991.

Claude, Richard P., Burns H. Weston (eds), *Human Rights in the World Community*, Philadelphia: University of Pennsylvania Press, 1989.

Crawford, James (ed.), *The Rights of Peoples*, Oxford: Clarendon Press, 1988.

Dijk, P. van, G. van Hoof, *Theory and Practice of the European Convention on Human Rights*, The Hague/London/Boston: Kluwer Law International, 3rd edn, 1998.

Donnelly, Jack, *Human Rights in Theory and Practice*, Ithaca/London: Cornell University Press, 1989.

Eide, Asbjørn, Jan Helgesen (eds), *The Future of Human Rights Protection in a Changing World: Fifty Years since the Four Freedoms Address; Essays in Honour of Torkel Opsahl*, Oslo: Norwegian University Press, 1991.

Eide, Asbjørn, Catarina Krause, Allan Rosas (eds), *Economic, Social and Cultural Rights: a Textbook*, Dordrecht/London/Boston: Martinus Nijhoff Publishers, 2nd edn, 2001.

Forsythe, David P. (ed.), *Human Rights in International Relations*, Cambridge: Cambridge University Press, 2000.

Forsythe, David P. (ed.), *Human Rights and Comparative Foreign Policy*, Tokyo: United Nations University Press, 2000.

Galenkamp, Marlies, *Individualism versus Collectivism: the Concept of Collective Rights*, Rotterdam: RFS, 1993.

Gomien, Donna (ed.), *Broadening the Frontiers of Human Rights: Essays in Honour of Asbjørn Eide*, Oslo: Oxford University Press, 1993.

Hayner, Priscilla B., *Unspeakable Truths: Confronting State Terror and Atrocity*, New York and London: Routledge, 2001.

Heijden, Barend van der and Bahia Tahrib-Lie (eds), *Reflections on the Universal Declaration of Human Rights: an Anthology*, The Hague/London/Boston: Martinus Nijhoff Publishers, 1998.

Howard, Rhoda E., *Human Rights and the Search for Community*, Boulder, Col.: Westview Press, 1995.

Lauren, Paul Gordon, *The Evolution of International Human Rights: Visions Seen*, Philadelphia: University of Pennsylvania Press, 1998.

Lawson, R.A., H.G. Schermers (eds), *Leading Cases of the European Court of Human Rights*, Nijmegen *et al.*: Ars Aequi Libri *et al.*, 1997.

Luard, Evan, *Human Rights and Foreign Policy*, Oxford: Pergamon Press, 1981.

Lutz, Ellen L., Hurst Hannum, Kathryn J. Burke (eds), *New Dimensions in Human Rights*, Philadelphia: University of Pennsylvania Press, 1989.

Mahoney E., P. Mahoney (eds), *Human Rights in the Twenty-First Century: a Global Challenge*, Dordrecht: Martinus Nijhoff Publishers, 1993.

Medina Quiroga, C., *The Battle of Human Rights: Gross Systematic Violations and the American System*, Dordrecht: Martinus Nijhoff Publishers, 1988.

Meron, Th. (ed.), *Human Rights in International Law: Legal and Political Issues*, Oxford: Clarendon Press, 1985.

Morsink, Johannes, *The Universal Declaration of Human Rights: Origins, Drafting & Intent*, Philadelphia: University of Pennsylvania Press, 1999.

Neuwahl, Nannette A., Allan Rosas (eds), *The European Union and Human Rights*, The Hague/London/Boston: Martinus Nijhoff Publishers, 1995.

Newman, Frank, David Weissbrodt, *International Human Rights: Law, Policy and Process*, Cincinnati, Ohio: Andersen, 1996.

Nowak, Manfred, *U.N. Covenant on Civil and Political Rights: CCPR Commentary*, Kehl/Strasbourg/Arlington: N.P. Engel Publishers, 1993.

Robertson, A.H., J.G. Merrills, *Human Rights in the World: an Introduction to the Study of the International Protection of Human Rights*, Manchester/New York: Manchester University Press, 4th edn, 1996.

Rodley, Nigel (ed.), *To Loose the Bands of Wickedness: International Intervention in Defence of Human Rights*, London: Brassey's, 1992.

Shute, Stephen, Susan Hurley (eds), *On Human Rights: the Oxford Amnesty Lectures 1993*, New York: Basic Books, 1993.

Tahzib, Bahiyyih G., *Freedom of Religion or Belief: Ensuring Effective International Legal Protection*, The Hague: Martinus Nijhoff Publishers, 1995.

Vincent, R.J., *Human Rights and International Relations*, Cambridge: Cambridge University Press, 1986.

Index